THE SOUTH AFRICAN
KETTLE BRAAI
COOKBOOK

THE SOUTH AFRICAN
KETTLE BRAAI
COOKBOOK

SHIRLEY GUY ■ MARTY KLINZMAN

Photography by Peter Brooks

ACKNOWLEDGEMENTS

We are indebted to the staff of Galactex for the loan
of all the barbeque equipment and to the suppliers
of Charka briquettes and fire-lighters which were
used for the testing of the recipes in this book.
Once again our thanks to Peter Brooks for his
patience during the photographic sessions.

Weber® is a registered trademark of
Weber Stephen Products Co. USA

First published by Struik Publishers (Pty) Ltd.
Editor: Linda de Villiers
Layout: Lellyn Creamer
Illustrator: Dave Snook
Photographer: Peter Brooks
Cover photographer: Alain Proust

Typesetting by Unifoto (Pty) Ltd, Cape Town
Reproduction done by PeterMAC Pre-Press cc.
Printed and bound by Shumani Printers (Pty) Ltd

ISBN 1 86825 415 1

Published by Cookbook Ink.
PO Box 85335 Emmarentia 2029

First published in 1990
First published in 1991
Second impression 1992
Second edition August 1993
Second impression December 1993
Third impression 1995
Fourth impression 1996
Fifth impression 1997
Sixth impression 2005

CONTENTS

Introduction **6**

Preparation **6**

Indirect Cooking **6**

Smoking Food in the Barbecue Kettle **7**

Direct Cooking **8**

Cleaning **8**

Problem Solver **9**

Successful Barbecuing **9**

Beef & Veal **11**

Lamb **23**

Game **33**

Pork **37**

Poultry **49**

Fish & Seafood **63**

Vegetables & Salads **75**

Salad Dressings, Sauces & Savoury Butters **88**

Desserts & Drinks **93**

Appetizers **100**

Breads & Batters **104**

Marinades **108**

Cooking Charts **109**

Popular Accessories **110**

Carving Meat & Poultry **110**

Index **112**

INTRODUCTION

Welcome to the wonderful world of barbecue kettles where you can barbecue year-round in any climate, producing delicious meals to be served either indoors or out. Meat, fish and poultry cooked on the barbecue kettle become succulent, golden brown and tender while vegetables remain great tasting.

For testing the recipes in this book, we used a 57cm (22¹/₂-in) diameter charcoal barbecue kettle and a gas kettle with a built-in lid. Gas kettles are available in various forms. Some look like large ovens and some are oval in shape. Most models take as little as 7 minutes to reach a temperature of 200 ºC (400 ºF). These gas kettles operate in the same way as the charcoal kettles, and consequently, the cooking times and cooking method specified in each recipe is similar. The cooking time should be increased slightly, and in smaller ovens the food should be turned once.

Over the years we have tested and developed a remarkable selection of delicious recipes which we feel will not only take the guesswork out of cooking on the barbecue kettle, but allow you, the host and hostess, to relax and enjoy the day too. We have included our favourite barbecue recipes for meat, fish, poultry and game as well as for vegetables, breads, desserts and appetizers. In addition there are recipes for mouthwatering marinades, sauces and savoury butters to enhance that traditional barbecue flavour we all love.

The advantages of kettle cooking far outweigh those of conventional barbecuing, for not only can foods be grilled and fried, but they can also be roasted, baked, braised, stewed and smoked. This versatility is accomplished by the use of two different cooking methods, namely the **direct** cooking method, which is the same as conventional barbecuing and is used primarily for foods which require fast cooking, and the **indirect** cooking method, where the kettle acts as a convection oven and is ideal for large roasts, baked hams, breads, baked desserts or anything that requires slow, even cooking. The latter method is used frequently in this book.

The temperature of the indirect fire is controlled by a number of factors,, namely the number of coals burning (that is, a 'normal' or a 'large' fire - see opposite), the outside temperature and whether the vents are open fully or not. Closing the vents slightly will decrease the temperature as this reduces the amount of oxygen drawn into the kettle and causes the coals to lose heat.

When you first start using the indirect cooking method, the temptation to 'peek' at the food will be very strong. Remember every time you do this, the barbecue kettle will be losing valuable heat. So if a turkey requires 3 hours to cook, don't lift the lid for at least 11/2 hours. As you gain more experience and confidence, you will know that the food is being cooked to perfection without the constant attention needed when barbecuing conventionally.

It is important that only charcoal briquettes are used in conjunction with fire-lighters because, while it is possible to use other types of fuel, you may find that the cooking times and the results vary a great deal from those stated in the recipes.

PREPARATION

INDIRECT COOKING

1. Open all the vents on the kettle and remove the lid.
2. Position the bottom (charcoal) grid so that the lines on the grid run in the same direction a the leg without the wheel. This will ensure that the air flows evenly around the food and out through the top vent. Now face the leg without a wheel into the wind.
3. Position the charcoal rails on either side of the grid, hooking them over the outside rails. The high side of the rails will then slip behind the third strut on the grid. (For a very much larger fire, position the charcoal rails one strut further towards the centre of the grid. For a very small fire, turn the rails around and hook them towards the centre of the grid, allowing them to slot into the strut of your choice.) If using a kettle with metal charcoal baskets, simply place them in position.
4. Place six briquettes on either side of the charcoal rails. Add two fire-lighters on top of the briquettes on each side.
5. Light the fire-lighters, making sure that they are all burning well, and allow them to burn for 3-4 minutes. Now add the remaining briquettes, for the size fire you require, to both sides. DO NOT REPLACE THE LID. Allow the fire to burn for at least 30 minutes. The fire is ready for use when the coals are red inside and covered with a fine layer of grey ash. No flames or smoke should be visible.
6. Place a foil drip pan between the two fire-beds to catch any fat, juice or baste which may fall from the food during cooking, then position the cooking grid with the handles over the coals.
7. Place the food on the grid directly over the drip pan and, unless otherwise directed, cover the kettle with the lid, placing the open vent in the same direction as the leg without a wheel.
8. Once the cooking is complete, close all the vents. The coals will go out and the remaining coals may be saved for future use. It is important, however, that when you make a new fire that no more than one-third of the coals should be 'used' ones as the heat they generate will be far less than normal.

Depending on the size of the food being cooked, you will need a NORMAL or a LARGE fire. When you first start cooking on the barbecue kettle, it is a good idea to count the number of coals needed to produce the required fire. With experience it becomes easy to judge.

	BRIQUETTES	BURNING TIME
LARGE FIRE	60-70 on each side	45 minutes
NORMAL FIRE	30-40 on each side	35 minutes

The burning time indicates how long it takes before the coals are ready for cooking.

NOTE: Please bear in mind that unless otherwise specified in the recipe, we have used a 'normal' fire to cook the food.

Roast chicken with roast potatoes and Farm-style sweetcorn (page 79)

Obviously the fire is at its hottest at the beginning of the cooking time. The heat will decrease gradually and eventually it will become low. It is helpful to know this if planning to cook more than one course on your barbecue kettle.

While it is possible to add extra briquettes during the cooking time, we have found that the best results are obtained when the fire is large enough to cook the food without adding extra briquettes. However, should it be necessary to stoke up the fire, remove the food and add more coals, allowing them to burn with the lid off for at least 10 minutes before replacing the food and continuing the cooking process. (Or use "ready" hot coals.)

SMOKING FOOD IN THE BARBECUE KETTLE
Wood chips, chunks or shavings may be used for smoking food in the barbecue kettle. While it is not essential to pre-soak these in water, we found that by doing so the chips, chunks or shavings lasted longer and gave the food a stronger smoked flavour. The smoking time will be slightly shorter if the chips are not soaked prior to adding them to the coals.

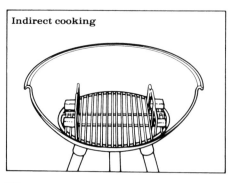

Position the charcoal grid and charcoal rails (steps **2** and **3** on page 6).

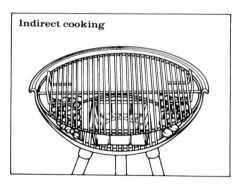

Place two fire-lighters on either side of the charcoal rails (step **4** on page 6).

Place a foil drip pan between the coals and position the cooking grid (step **6** on page 6).

Place food on the cooking grid directly over the drip pan. Cover the kettle (step **7** on page 6).

Add a heap of briquettes about 2-3 minutes after igniting fire-lighters (steps **3** and **4** below).

When coals are covered with a layer of ash, place food in the centre of the cooking grid (step **5** below).

PREPARATION OF THE BARBECUE KETTLE FOR DIRECT COOKING

1. Open all the vents, then remove the lid.

2. Position the bottom grid so that the lines on the grid run in the same direction as the leg without a wheel.

3. Place 2-3 fire-lighters in the **centre** of the charcoal grid and add 10 briquettes.

4. Ignite the fire-lighters and after 2-3 minutes add a heap of briquettes (take care not to smother the fire-lighters) and allow them to burn until they are red with a fine layer of grey ash. The number of coals in this case will depend on how much food is to be barbecued. To prepare a fire for direct cooking, arrange the briquettes in a pyramid shape, and when the coals are ready for cooking spread them out slightly, using a pair of long-handled tongs.

If a smaller fire is required, place the charcoal rails in position by hooking them over the outside rails. The high side of the rails will then slip behind the third strut on the grid. In the case of direct cooking, the charcoal rails keep the coals in the centre of the charcoal grid.

Meat may be cooked with or without the lid in position, but we do not recommend that you cook meat with a lot of fat on it with the lid on as the burning fat causes a large build-up of grease inside the kettle.

5. Position the cooking grid and place the food in the centre of the grid.

6. Once the cooking is complete, close all the vents to ex-tinguish the fire. The remaining briquettes may be saved for future use. However, it is important that no more than one-third of the coals should be 'used' ones as the heat they generate will be far less than normal.

NOTE: Never use petrol, benzine or any other flammable liquids when lighting your barbecue kettle.

CLEANING

1. Wait until the kettle is completely cool before cleaning it.

2. Remove the cooking grid and charcoal grid. Move the vent handle back and forth to remove the ash. The ash will fall into the ash catcher which can then be emptied.

3. Scrub the cooking grid with a brass wire brush, using hot sudsy water and a scouring agent. If you do not have a suitable brush, use a crumpled-up ball of foil.

4. Remove the drip pan and wash it, then set it aside for future use.

5. It is not necessary to clean the entire barbecue after each use, simply wipe the inside of the lid and replace. However, when a thorough cleaning is necessary use a soft wire brush and plenty of hot sudsy water. Oven cleaner may also be used.

6. Never spray cold water onto a hot barbecue kettle as this will damage the enamelled surface.

NOTE: Gas barbecue kettles are easy to clean as most of the oven parts are dishwasher-proof.

PROBLEM SOLVER

PROBLEM • Food cooks too slowly and does not have a good brown colour.

REASON • Briquettes were not allowed to burn long enough before adding the food and covering the kettle with the lid.
• Too few coals.
• The vents may not be sufficiently open or the bottom vent may be blocked with ash.
• Incorrect type of briquettes is being used.
• Kettle may be situated in an extremely windy position.

SOLUTION • Allow coals to turn completely to ash before you begin cooking.
• Add the correct number of briquettes as specified on page 6.
• Open the top and bottom vents when lighting the fire. If the vents are blocked, remove the cooking grid, coals, charcoal rails and grid, and brush the ash through the open vents into the ash catcher. Some models allow the user to remove accumulated ash without having to remove the internal grids.
• Use the type of briquettes recommended by the manufacturer of your barbecue kettle.
• Move the kettle to a more sheltered position.

PROBLEM • Oil or fat dripping into ash catcher.

REASON • No drip pan in position.
• Very fatty foods being cooked with the lid on and over a direct fire.

SOLUTION • Using oven gloves, remove food and cooking grid. Position a drip pan or pans between the coals. Replace grid and food.
• Trim off excess fat or use indirect cooking method in future.

PROBLEM • Food tastes of paraffin.

REASON • Fire-lighters were still burning when food was placed in kettle.
• Briquettes were insufficiently burned before adding the food.

SOLUTION • Discard the food. In future, ensure that the fire-lighters have completely burned away and the coals have turned to ash before you start cooking.

PROBLEM • One side of the fire goes out when cooking indirectly.

REASON • The charcoal grid and fire-bed were not correctly placed over the vents.

SOLUTION • Using oven gloves, reposition the charcoal grid and rails correctly. Using tongs, replace the coals and leave the lid off until both fires have ashed over.

PROBLEM • Fire-lighters go out before igniting the charcoal briquettes.

REASON • Briquettes are old and crumbly or damp.
• Fire-lighters are old and dry.

SOLUTION • Remove the briquettes and replace with new or dry ones. Allow damp briquettes to dry before re-using them.
• Replace with new, fresh fire-lighters.

PROBLEM • Food is scorched on the base and sides when using the indirect cooking method.

REASON • Food is too large and hangs over the coals.

SOLUTION • If cooking a particularly large joint, make the two sides of the fire narrower (Step 3 of Preparing a fire for indirect cooking). Shield the sides and top of the food by covering it loosely with foil and half close the vents.

PROBLEM • Vegetables or desserts do not cook in the stipulated time.

REASON • By the time you are ready to cook the vegetables or dessert, the coals may have been burning for a couple of hours and will have lost some of their heat.

SOLUTION • Add a few more coals and allow 10 minutes before adding the food.

SUCCESSFUL BARBECUING

These simple rules will help you master the secret of successful cooking in the barbecue kettle.

DO'S

• Do cover the kettle when cooking unless directed otherwise.
• Do seal and brown the meat with the lid off when cooking by the direct method. Hang the kettle lid on the handle using the hook inside the lid.
• Do leave the kettle lid off while starting the fire.
• Do ensure that all the vents are open before lighting the fire.
• Do ensure that the grid is in the correct position before preparing the fire.
• Do make sure that the coals are coated with ash before adding the food and covering the kettle.

DON'TS

• Do not use flammable liquids with briquettes.
• Do not spray the hot barbecue kettle with water.
• Do not 'peek' at the food during cooking time. This will result in considerable heat loss and lengthen the cooking time.
• Do not use treated or painted woods for smoking food on the barbecue kettle.
• Do not cook very fatty foods over a direct fire with the lid on.
• Do not move the kettle with the lid on as it may fall off and chip.
• Do not place a hot lid on the lawn or any other surface which could be damaged by heat.
• Do not light the fire or cook indoors.

BEEF & VEAL

Charcoal-flavoured beef has been a favourite since the barbecue gained popularity. Tender sizzling steaks, juicy hamburgers, delicious kebabs and roasts remain choice barbecue fare.

To ensure even cooking, it is best to bring steaks and smaller beef cuts to room temperature before placing them on the barbecue. Trim excess fat from steaks and slash remaining fat at 2-cm (¾-in) intervals to prevent the meat from curling. To test if the meat is cooked to the desired degree of rareness, make a tiny slit in the centre of small cuts of meat. A meat thermometer is invaluable for checking larger cuts; insert the thermometer in the thickest part of the meat, away from the bone. Remove large cuts before they are completely cooked, and allow them to stand for a few minutes before carving so that the juices can settle back in the tissues.

Lean cuts of beef will benefit from a marinade or basting sauce to keep them succulent, and to enhance the flavour.

For a change of pace, try smoking the meat, and add water or other liquids such as wine, fruit juices and beer to the drip pan to ensure the meat remains juicy.

Allow 200 g (7 oz) of beef per person or 300 g (11 oz) for those with hearty appetites.

Perfect rump (page 20), Pastrami (page 14),
Butternut squash with cumin (page 82)
and Yorkshire pudding (page 104)

STUFFED FILLET (Serves 6-8)

Indirect . . . 30 minutes. Roast holder.

INGREDIENTS	METRIC/IMPERIAL	AMERICAN
beef fillet, trimmed	1.5 kg (3 lb)	3 lb
salt and black pepper		
melted butter	30 ml (2 tbsp)	2 tbsp
STUFFING		
canned smoked oysters	100 g (3½ oz)	½ cup
fresh breadcrumbs	60 g (2 oz)	1 cup
chopped parsley	45 ml (3 tbsp)	3 tbsp
dried thyme	2.5 ml (½ tsp)	½ tsp
salt and black pepper		
butter	30 ml (2 tbsp)	2 tbsp
onion, chopped	1 small	1 small
dry sherry	30 ml (2 tbsp)	2 tbsp
sour cream	45 ml (3 tbsp)	3 tbsp

First make the stuffing: Combine oysters, bread-crumbs, parsley, thyme, salt and pepper. Melt the butter and sauté the onion, add to oyster mixture along with the sherry and cream, mixing well.

Make an incision down one side of the fillet (or use a sharpening steel to make a hole down the middle) and stuff the meat. Using a needle and thread, sew up the opening if the meat has been cut. Tie with string to keep in shape. Season lightly and brush with butter.

Prepare an indirect fire and fit a foil drip pan between the coals. Place meat in a roast holder and position it on the grid over the drip pan. Cover the kettle and cook for 25-30 minutes, depending on the degree of rareness required. Stand for a few minutes before carving.

ROAST LEG OF VEAL (Serves 10)

Indirect . . . 2¼ hours. Roast holder.

INGREDIENTS	METRIC/IMPERIAL	AMERICAN
leg or part of a leg of veal	2.5 kg (5½ lb)	5½ lb
vegetable oil	30 ml (2 tbsp)	2 tbsp
salt and black pepper		
fresh marjoram	large sprig	large sprig
redcurrant jelly	100 g (3½ oz)	⅓ cup

Rub the meat with oil and then season well. Place in a roast holder and top with herbs.

Prepare an indirect fire and fit a foil drip pan between the coals. Place the meat on the grid above the drip pan, then cover the kettle and cook for about 1¾ hours. Heat redcurrant jelly and brush the meat generously. Cover and cook for another 30 minutes, brushing with the jelly once more during this time.

CHAMPAGNE SAUSAGE
(Makes about 1 kg / 2¼ lb)

Direct . . . 15-20 minutes.

INGREDIENTS	METRIC/IMPERIAL	AMERICAN
beef chuck	450 g (1 lb)	1 lb
loin of pork	300 g (11 oz)	11 oz
pork fat	225 g (8 oz)	8 oz
garlic, crushed	2 cloves	2 cloves
chopped onion	45 ml (3 tbsp)	3 tbsp
dried marjoram	2.5 ml (½ tsp)	½ tsp
paprika	2.5 ml (½ tsp)	½ tsp
ground cloves	pinch	pinch
salt	10 ml (2 tsp)	2 tsp
black pepper	2.5 ml (½ tsp)	½ tsp
chopped walnuts	60 ml (4 tbsp)	4 tbsp
dry sparkling wine	75 ml (2½ fl oz)	⅓ cup
sausage casings	about 2 m (6½ ft)	about 6½ ft

Cut meat and fat into strips. Freeze for about 30 minutes, then mince (grind) through the fine blade of a meat mincer (grinder). Mix in garlic, onion, seasonings and walnuts. Stir in sparkling wine a little at a time, then chill for about 1 hour. Stuff casings with meat mixture, then let dry in the refrigerator for at least 12 hours or up to 24 hours.

To cook: Prepare a direct fire, then arrange the sausage in coils and place them on the grid over medium-low coals. Cook slowly for 15-20 minutes, or to desired degree of rareness, turning occasionally.

SMOKED ROAST BEEF (Serves 8-10)

Indirect . . . 2-2½ hours

The beef has a smoky flavour with a touch of wine.

INGREDIENTS	METRIC/IMPERIAL	AMERICAN
rump roast, tied into shape	about 2 kg (4½ lb)	about 4½ lb
dry red wine	200 ml (7 fl oz)	¾ cup
brown sugar	30 ml (2 tbsp)	2 tbsp
Worcestershire sauce	15 ml (1 tbsp)	1 tbsp
water	1 litre (1¾ pints)	4 cups
bacon	8 rashers	8 slices
smoke chips, soaked	175 g (6 oz)	3 cups
VEGETABLES		
potatoes, unpeeled and quartered	4	4
carrots, cut into 6-cm (2½-in) lengths	6	6
onions, halved	4 large	4 large
water		
garlic, crushed	2 cloves	2 cloves
salt and black pepper		

To prepare the meat: Combine 60 ml (4 tbsp) wine, the brown sugar and Worcestershire sauce and mix well. Rub mixture into the meat and wrap tightly in cling wrap. Refrigerate overnight or up to 24 hours.

Prepare a *large* indirect fire, fit a foil drip pan between the coals and add remaining wine and the water.

Place potatoes, carrots and onions in a disposable foil dish and add water to half fill the dish. Sprinkle with garlic and salt and pepper.

Place roast in the roast holder and top with the bacon. Sprinkle water-soaked smoke chips over the coals, place the roast holder over the drip pan and the vegetables on the side directly over the coals. Cover the kettle and cook for 2-2½ hours, depending on desired degree of rareness of the meat. Add more water and wine to the drip pan as needed, and more hot coals and soaked smoke chips as necessary.

To serve: Remove bacon and carve beef thinly. Serve with the smoked vegetables.

FILLET WITH GREEN PEPPERCORN BÉARNAISE (Serves 6-8)

Indirect . . . 30 minutes. Roast holder.

INGREDIENTS	METRIC/IMPERIAL	AMERICAN
beef fillet	1.5 kg (3 lb)	3 lb
a little Italian olive oil		
salt and black pepper		
fresh herbs	small bunch	small bunch
GREEN PEPPER- CORN BÉARNAISE		
egg yolks	3	3
spring (green) onion	1	1
salt	2.5 ml (½ tsp)	½ tsp
white pepper	pinch	pinch
white wine vinegar	10 ml (2 tsp)	2 tsp
dry white wine	45 ml (3 tbsp)	3 tbsp
butter	125 g (4 oz)	½ cup
dried green peppercorns	10-15 ml (2-3 tsp)	2-3 tsp

Rub the fillet with oil and sprinkle with salt and pepper. Place in a roast holder and top with a small bunch of fresh herbs.

Prepare an indirect fire and fit a foil drip pan between the coals. Place the roast holder on the grid over the drip pan. Cover the kettle and cook for 20-30 minutes, depending on the size and thickness of the meat. Stand for 5 minutes before carving into 6-mm (¼-in) thick slices and serving with Green Peppercorn Béarnaise.

To make the Béarnaise: Fit the metal blade to the work bowl of a food processor, place yolks, spring onion, salt and pepper, vinegar and wine into the bowl. Process for 45 seconds. Heat the butter until boiling, then with the motor running, slowly add the butter through the feed tube and process for about 50 seconds. Add peppercorns and process for a few seconds longer. The sauce may be kept warm for a short time over hot water, or it may be reheated on 30% in the microwave, stirring every 30 seconds, until heated through.

VEAL CHOPS WITH SAGE AND ROSEMARY (Serves 6)

Indirect . . . about 12 minutes.

INGREDIENTS	METRIC/IMPERIAL	AMERICAN
veal chops, 3-cm (1¼-in) thick	6	6
vegetable oil	250 ml (9 fl oz)	1 cup
chopped fresh sage	60 ml (4 tbsp)	4 tbsp
chopped fresh rosemary	30 ml (2 tbsp)	2 tbsp
garlic, finely crushed	3 cloves	3 cloves
fresh sage and rosemary sprigs		
salt and pepper		

Combine oil, chopped sage and rosemary and garlic, mixing well. Pour over veal chops and marinate, refrigerated, for at least 4 hours, or up to two days.

To cook: Prepare an indirect fire and place a foil drip pan between the coals. Soak sage and rosemary sprigs in water for 10 minutes. Place damp herbs in the drip pan. Drain chops and season with salt and pepper. Place on the grid over the drip pan, cover the kettle and cook for 5-6 minutes per side for medium rare, brushing with marinade occasionally.

CARPETBAG STEAK (Serves 3-4)

Direct . . . 10 minutes

INGREDIENTS	METRIC/IMPERIAL	AMERICAN
rump, cut 4-cm (1½-in) thick	1 slice	1 slice
fresh oysters	12	12
oyster sauce	30 ml (2 tbsp)	2 tbsp
butter	15 ml (1 tbsp)	1 tbsp
salt and black pepper		
olive oil		

Cut a pocket into the side of the steak. Combine oysters, oyster sauce, butter and a little black pepper. Stuff the mixture into the pocket, secure with poultry skewers (pins) and brush with oil. Season the steak lightly.

Prepare a direct fire and when the coals are dull, place the meat on the grid. Cover the kettle and cook for 4-5 minutes on each side. Serve with herb butter.

MEAT LOAF (Serves 6)

Indirect . . . 45 minutes

INGREDIENTS	METRIC/IMPERIAL	AMERICAN
vegetable oil	15 ml (1 tbsp)	1 tbsp
onion, chopped	1 small	1 small
minced (ground) topside	750 g (1½ lb)	1½ lb
fresh breadcrumbs	30 g (1 oz)	½ cup
garlic, crushed	1 clove	1 clove
dried mixed herbs	5 ml (1 tsp)	1 tsp
egg	1	1
beef stock	100 ml (3½ fl oz)	½ cup
tomato sauce	60 ml (4 tbsp)	4 tbsp
H P sauce	15 ml (1 tbsp)	1 tbsp
Worcestershire sauce	10 ml (2 tsp)	2 tsp
salt and black pepper		
dry mustard	5 ml (1 tsp)	1 tsp

Heat the oil and sauté the onion for a few seconds. Combine onions with remaining ingredients and pack into an oiled 25 x 10-cm (10 x 4-in) loaf tin.

Prepare an indirect fire and place the loaf tin in the centre of the grid. Cover the kettle and cook for 45 minutes. Serve hot or cold.

MARINATED STEAKS (Serves 8)

Direct . . . 11-15 minutes.

INGREDIENTS	METRIC/IMPERIAL	AMERICAN
rump, rib eye, or club steaks, 3-cm (1¼-in) thick	8 portions	8 portions
MARINADE		
dry red wine	190 ml (6½ fl oz)	¾ cup
onion, chopped	1 large	1 large
chopped parsley	45 g (1½ oz)	½ cup
garlic, chopped	2 cloves	2 cloves
bay leaf, crumbled	1	1
dried tarragon	5 ml (1 tsp)	1 tsp
dried thyme	5 ml (1 tsp)	1 tsp
black pepper	2.5 ml (½ tsp)	½ tsp
Tabasco sauce	few drops	few drops

Slash fat to keep meat from curling on the kettle. Make the marinade by combining all ingredients. Place meat in a large plastic bag, add marinade and seal bag. Marinate for 4 hours, turning occasionally.

Prepare a direct fire. Place the meat on a lightly oiled grid and cook to desired degree of rareness. Calculate the cooking time for rare steak as 5 minutes on one side, 6 minutes on the second side; for medium as 7 minutes on the first side, about 8 minutes on the second. Baste frequently with the marinade during cooking time.

ISLAND BEEF KEBABS (Serves 4)

Direct . . . 10 minutes

INGREDIENTS	METRIC/IMPERIAL	AMERICAN
sirloin	750 g (1½ lb)	1½ lb
desiccated coconut	100 g (3½ oz)	1 cup
boiling water	125 ml (4 fl oz)	½ cup
freshly grated root ginger	2.5 ml (½ tsp)	½ tsp
crushed dried chilli pepper	5 ml (1 tsp)	1 tsp
vegetable oil	60 ml (4 tbsp)	4 tbsp
light rum	60 ml (4 tbsp)	4 tbsp
garlic, peeled	1 clove	1 clove
onions, cooked	12 small	12 small
oranges, peeled and quartered	2	2
small pineapple, peeled and cubed	1	1

Cut meat into 3-cm (1¼-in) cubes. Place 75 g (2½ oz) desiccated coconut in a bowl. Pour boiling water over and leave to stand until cool. Then strain, pressing out all liquid.

Combine coconut liquid, remaining desiccated coconut, ginger, chilli pepper, oil and rum. Place meat in a glass bowl and pour coconut mixture over. Place garlic in the centre, cover and chill for about 4 hours. Drain meat, reserving marinade. Thread meat, onions, oranges and pineapple chunks onto four skewers.

Prepare a direct fire and when coals are medium hot, cook the kebabs for 8-10 minutes, turning and brushing with marinade occasionally.

PASTRAMI (Serves 8)

Indirect . . . 2½ hours. Roast holder.

INGREDIENTS	METRIC/IMPERIAL	AMERICAN
raw, ready-prepared pastrami (cured beef)	1.5 kg (3 lb)	3 lb
cooking bag		

Prepare an indirect fire and fit a foil drip pan between the coals. Place the meat in a large cooking bag and tie the end loosely to allow the steam to escape. Place meat in a roast holder on the grid over the drip pan. Half close the vents top and bottom to reduce the heat, as pastrami requires longer, slower cooking than most beef dishes. Cover the kettle and cook for 2-2½ hours. Open the vents after 1 hour if the fire seems to be slowing down too much. Stand the meat for 15 minutes before serving. Slice thinly and serve with Mustard Sauce (page 89).

Island beef kebabs, Sweetcorn salad (page 87) and Baked apple slices (page 94)

STEAK WITH SPICY TOMATO SAUCE
(Serves 4)

Direct . . . 13 minutes

INGREDIENTS	METRIC/IMPERIAL	AMERICAN
rump or porterhouse steaks, cut 2-cm (¾-in) thick	4	4
salt		
MARINADE		
onion, chopped	1 large	1 large
tomato sauce	250 ml (9 fl oz)	1 cup
Worcestershire sauce	30 ml (2 tbsp)	2 tbsp
H P sauce	30 ml (2 tbsp)	2 tbsp
black pepper		
brown vinegar	45 ml (3 tbsp)	3 tbsp
cayenne pepper	pinch	pinch

First make the marinade: Combine all the ingredients and pour into a shallow pan. Add the steaks and turn to coat. Marinate for at least 3 hours. Remove the steak and pat dry with paper towel.

Prepare a direct fire, heat a cast-iron griddle or frying pan until a blue haze forms. Sprinkle with a little salt. Dry-fry the steaks for 3-4 minutes per side, turning the meat once only. Remove steaks and keep warm. Add marinade to the pan or griddle and cook for 5 minutes, stirring all the time. Should the marinade become too thick, add a little water. Pour over the steaks and serve at once.

SAUERBRATEN (Serves 10-12)

Indirect . . . 1 hour 40 minutes

INGREDIENTS	METRIC/IMPERIAL	AMERICAN
rump or sirloin roast	about 2.5 kg (5½ lb)	about 5½ lb
wine vinegar	500 ml (18 fl oz)	2¼ cups
water	500 ml (18 fl oz)	2¼ cups
brown sugar	60 ml (4 tbsp)	4 tbsp
salt	15 ml (1 tbsp)	1 tbsp
black pepper	2.5 ml (½ tsp)	½ tsp
ground cloves	2.5 ml (½ tsp)	½ tsp
bay leaf	1	1
onions, chopped	3	3
carrots, diced	2 large	2 large
celery, chopped	4 sticks	4 stalks
vegetable oil	30 ml (2 tbsp)	2 tbsp
ginger biscuits (cookies), crumbled	9	9

Place meat in a large bowl. Combine remaining ingredients, except oil and biscuits, and pour over the meat. Cover and refrigerate for 2-3 days, turning meat several times.

To cook: Remove meat from marinade and pat dry. Brown the meat on all sides in a little oil in a large cast-iron casserole. Add marinade and vegetables.

Prepare an indirect fire and place the casserole directly over the hot coals to bring the liquid to the boil, then position in the centre of the grid. Cover the casserole and the kettle and cook for about 20 minutes per 450 g (1 lb) - about 1 hour 40 minutes or to desired degree of rareness of the meat. Remove meat and keep warm.

For the gravy: Strain the liquid into a 1-litre (1¾-pints/4-cup) measure, discarding the vegetables. Allow liquid to cool for a few minutes, then skim off fat, reserving about 60 ml (4 tbsp). Add fat to the casserole, stir in 500 ml (18 fl oz/2¼ cups) of the liquid and sprinkle in the ginger biscuits. Cook, stirring, until mixture thickens and is bubbly. Slice the meat and serve with the gravy.

SMOKED RIBS AMERICAN-STYLE
(Serves 6-8)

Indirect . . . 35 minutes. Rib rack.

INGREDIENTS	METRIC/IMPERIAL	AMERICAN
pork ribs	4 large strips	4 large strips
vegetable oil	30 ml (2 tbsp)	2 tbsp
onions, chopped	2	2
garlic	1-2 cloves	1-2 cloves
beef stock	250 ml (9 fl oz)	1 cup
brown vinegar	100 ml (3½ fl oz)	½ cup
ground ginger	2.5 ml (½ tsp)	½ tsp
tomato purée	75 ml (2½ fl oz)	⅓ cup
tomato sauce	75 ml (2½ fl oz)	⅓ cup
American chilli powder	5 ml (1 tsp)	1 tsp
brown sugar	30 ml (2 tbsp)	2 tbsp
fruit chutney	75 ml (2½ fl oz)	⅓ cup
salt and black pepper		
sherry	45 ml (3 tbsp)	3 tbsp
smoke chips (preferably mesquite), soaked	15 ml (1 tbsp)	1 tbsp

Heat the oil and sauté onions and garlic. Add remaining ingredients, except ribs and smoke chips, and simmer for 20 minutes. Allow to cool. Place trimmed ribs in a large shallow dish and pour marinade over. Stand overnight.

Prepare an indirect fire and fit a foil drip pan between the coals. Place the ribs in a rib rack and then onto the gird above the drip pan. Cover the kettle and cook for 25 minutes. Baste the meat with the marinade and sprinkle soaked smoke chips on each side of the fire. Cover the kettle, close the top vents, and cook for another 10 minutes. Cut into riblets and serve.

Smoked ribs American-style and
Savoury beer loaf (page 107)

STEAK FAJITAS (Serves 6-8)

Direct . . . 15 minutes. Cooking (Manchurian) grill.

An excellent dish to make for a large number of people.

INGREDIENTS	METRIC/IMPERIAL	AMERICAN
rump steak	about 1 kg (2¼ lb)	about 2½ lb
vegetable oil	45 ml (3 tbsp)	3 tbsp
onions, sliced	2	2
Tortillas*		
FAJITAS MARINADE		
orange juice	250 ml (9 fl oz)	1 cup
vegetable oil	125 ml (4 fl oz)	½ cup
red wine	60 ml (4 tbsp)	4 tbsp
lemon juice	60 ml (4 tbsp)	4 tbsp
cayenne pepper	large pinch	large pinch
black pepper	2.5 ml (½ tsp)	½ tsp
ground cumin	1 ml (¼ tsp)	¼ tsp
garlic, crushed	2 cloves	2 cloves
GUACAMOLE		
avocados	2	2
chopped onion	30 ml (2 tbsp)	2 tbsp
green chillies, chopped	1-2 small	1-2 small
chopped fresh coriander (cilantro)	10 ml (2 tsp)	2 tsp
lemon juice	10 ml (2 tsp)	2 tsp
salt and black pepper		
SALSA		
tomatoes, chopped	2 large	2 large
onion, chopped	1 small	1 small
green chillies, chopped	1-2	1-2
chopped parsley	15 ml (1 tbsp)	1 tbsp
lemon juice	15 ml (1 tbsp)	1 tbsp
salt and black pepper		

First make the fajitas marinade: Lightly whisk together the ingredients, place the meat in a shallow dish and pour marinade over. Stand overnight, turning occasionally. Drain meat and pat dry.

Prepare a direct fire, then fit the cooking grill and allow to become hot. Add oil and heat for a few seconds. Fry the onions until well browned, then remove and set aside. Scrape the pan well and fry the steak for a few minutes on each side. The meat should be brown, but the flesh should be pink inside. Carve the meat thinly across the grain. Combine with onions and serve with tortillas, guacamole and salsa.

To make guacamole: Blend all the ingredients together. To make the salsa: Combine all the ingredients.

* Available from some supermarkets and speciality stores.

FILET AU POIVRE (Serves 6)

Indirect . . . 45-54 minutes.

Tender fillet of beef, grilled whole and cut into succulent slices.

INGREDIENTS	METRIC/IMPERIAL	AMERICAN
whole beef fillet	1.5 kg (3 lb)	3 lb
combined green, white and black peppercorns, coarsely crushed	30 ml (2 tbsp)	2 tbsp
fresh herbs, chopped	10 ml (2 tsp)	2 tsp
back bacon, thickly sliced	8-10 rashes	8-10 slices
butter, melted	100 g (3½ oz)	⅓ cup
brandy	60 ml (4 tbsp)	4 tbsp
salt		

Trim the fillet, removing tail and scraggy bits, and reserve for another use. Rub peppercorns into the meat and stand for at least 30 minutes at room temperature or about 3 hours in the refrigerator. Pat herbs onto the meat. Cover with the bacon and tie at intervals.

Prepare an indirect fire and place a foil drip pan between the coals. Place the meat on a well-oiled grid over the drip pan. Cover the kettle and cook for about 10-12 minutes per 450 g (1 lb) for medium rare or 12-16 minutes per 450 g (1 lb) for medium. Remove and stand for about 10 minutes before carving.

To serve hot, carve into eight slices. Pour a little butter over the beef. Heat the brandy, set alight and pour over the meat. To serve cold, let cool, then chill and slice thinly. Season with salt just before serving.

STANDING RIB ROAST (Serves 8-10)

Indirect . . . 2 hours. Roast holder.

INGREDIENTS	METRIC/IMPERIAL	AMERICAN
rib roast on the bone	2-2.5 kg (4½-5½ lb)	4½-5½ lb
vegetable oil	30 ml (2 tbsp)	2 tbsp
salt and black pepper		
fresh marjoram	large sprigs	large sprigs

Rub meat with oil and season lightly with salt and pepper. Top with herbs, then place in a roast holder with the fat side uppermost.

Prepare an indirect fire and fit a drip pan between the coals. Place meat on the grid above the drip pan, cover the kettle and cook for 1½-2 hours. Stand for 10 minutes before carving into 6-mm (½-in) thick slices. Serve with Yorkshire Pudding (page 104).

Steak fajitas and Sweetcorn parcels (page 79)

BOLOGNESE SAUCE (Serves 8)

Direct . . . 65 minutes

INGREDIENTS	METRIC/IMPERIAL	AMERICAN
spicy sausage, cubed	500 g (18 oz)	3 cups
vegetable oil	60 ml (4 tbsp)	4 tbsp
minced (ground) beef	1 kg (2¼ lb)	2¼ lb
onion, chopped	1	1
garlic, crushed	1-2 cloves	1-2 cloves
green pepper, diced	1	1
celery, chopped	3 sticks	3 stalks
canned whole peeled tomatoes	1.5 kg (3½ lb)	3½ lb
bay leaf	1	1
dried oregano	30 ml (2 tbsp)	2 tbsp
dried basil	20 ml (4 tsp)	4 tsp
or fresh, chopped	60 ml (4 tbsp)	4 tbsp
salt	10 ml (2 tsp)	2 tsp
black pepper	5 ml (1 tsp)	1 tsp
dry red wine	250 ml (9 fl oz)	1 cup
canned tomato paste	230 g (8 oz)	8 oz
ground mixed spice	large pinch	large pinch
Tabasco sauce (optional)	few drops	few drops

Prepare a direct fire. Brown sausage in oil in a heavy cast-iron casserole over hot coals, then remove with a slotted spoon. Add beef, onion, garlic, green pepper, and celery and cook, stirring, until beef has browned. Add sausage, tomatoes with liquid, bay leaf, herbs, salt and pepper. Cover the casserole and the kettle and cook for 30-40 minutes, stirring occasionally. Add wine, tomato paste, mixed spice, and Tabasco sauce, if using. Mix well, cover the casserole and the kettle and cook for about 15 minutes more. Stand for 30 minutes before serving or, if possible, chill overnight, then reheat.

PERFECT RUMP (Serves 15)

Indirect . . . 1¼ hours. Roast holder.

INGREDIENTS	METRIC/IMPERIAL	AMERICAN
whole matured rump	3 kg (7 lb)	7 lb
vegetable oil	30 ml (2 tbsp)	2 tbsp
salt and black pepper		
fresh marjoram	large sprig	large sprig

Rub the meat well with oil, salt and pepper. Prepare an indirect fire and fit a foil drip pan between the coals. Place meat in a roast holder and top with marjoram. Place the meat on the grid above the drip pan, cover the kettle and cook for 1-1¼ hours, depending on the degree of rareness required. Stand for 5 minutes before carving. Serve with Pan-baked Potato Slices (page 76) or Yorkshire Pudding (page 104).

Hamburgers and Bolognese sauce on spaghetti

HAMBURGERS ON THE BARBECUE
(Makes 6 Hamburgers)

Direct . . . 8 minutes.

The ideal hamburger uses about 175 g (6 oz/1¼ cups) minced (ground) beef. Use meat with some fat content for juicy burgers, and handle the meat as little as possible, both during the shaping of the patties (cakes) and during the cooking.

INGREDIENTS	METRIC/IMPERIAL	AMERICAN
minced (ground) beef	1 kg (2¼ lb)	2¼ lb
salt	2.5-5 ml (½-1 tsp)	½-1 tsp
pepper		

Mix beef and seasoning together gently and shape into six patties.

Prepare a direct fire and place patties on a well-oiled grid over medium coals. Cook for 2 minutes to sear, then

gently turn and cook 4-6 minutes more, depending on desired degree of rareness.

VARIATIONS
Any of the following may be added to the beef.
* Blue cheese - use about 60 ml (4 tbsp) grated cheese per 1 kg (2¼ lb) meat. Omit the salt.
* 2.5-5 ml (½-1 tsp) prepared horseradish per 1 kg (2¼ lb) meat.
* 5-7.5 ml (1-1½ tsp) Worcestershire sauce; a few drops Tabasco sauce and 30 ml (2 tbsp) finely chopped onion per 1 kg (2¼ lb) meat.

Californian burger: Combine 125 g (4 oz/½ cup) mashed ripe avocado, 3 grated radishes, pinch salt, 15 ml (1 tbsp) lemon juice and few drops Tabasco sauce, mixing well. Place cooked patty on bottom of toasted hamburger roll and top with avocado mixture.

Bombay burger: First make the chickpea topping: Heat 15 ml (1 tbsp) oil, and sauté 30 g (1 oz/⅓ cup) finely chopped onion until soft. Add 5 ml (1 tsp) curry powder (or to taste), pinch ground cumin, mix well and cook 1 minute. Drain 400 g (14 oz) canned chickpeas and mash half of them. Add mashed and whole chickpeas and 75 ml (2½ fl oz/⅓ cup) water to the onion mixture. Heat through, stirring occasionally. Slide cooked patty into a pitta bread, then add chickpea topping.

Hamburg burger: Top each patty with a slice of Emmenthal cheese during the last 2 minutes of cooking time. Place patties on buttered rye bread and top with heated, drained sauerkraut, dollops of sour cream and a second slice of rye bread.

Smoky burgers: Combine 250 ml (9 fl oz/1 cup) tomato sauce, 60 ml (4 tbsp) Worcestershire sauce, 30 ml (2 tbsp) butter, 5 ml (1 tsp) sugar, 5 ml (1 tsp) salt, 2.5 ml (½ tsp) pepper and 2.5 ml (½ tsp) instant coffee. Heat to boiling. Combine 60 ml (4 tbsp) of this sauce with ½ small chopped onion. Shape 750 g (1½ lb) beef into 12 thin patties. Spoon a little of the onion mixture on 6 patties, top with remaining patties and seal edges well.

Prepare a direct fire and sprinkle 90 g (3 oz/1½ cups) soaked smoke chips over the coals. Place patties on the oiled grid, cover tne kettle and cook for about 7 minutes. Turn patties and cook for a further 7 minutes. Place buttered rolls, buttered side up, around the edge of the kettle during the last 3-4 minutes. Brush patties with remaining sauce and serve on rolls. (Serves 6)

LAMB

There is nothing to compare with the flavour of barbecued lamb. Along with traditional lamb chops, cutlets (ribs) and kebabs, a leg of lamb lends itself beautifully to the barbecue kettle. The crispy brown crust encloses juicy, slightly pink, flavoursome meat that melts in the mouth. Lamb is versatile and delicious whether barbecued simply or with the addition of marinades and glazes. A heated and oiled grid will prevent the meat from sticking.

Leg of lamb in buttermilk (page 28), Sweet and sour lamb ribs (page 25) and Stuffed gem squash (page 76)

LAMB WITH HERBS (Serves 6-8)

Indirect . . . 1½ hours. Roast holder

A spicy dish, with a beautiful well-flavoured garlic sauce.

INGREDIENTS	METRIC/IMPERIAL	AMERICAN
leg of lamb	1.5-2 kg (3-4½ lb)	3-4½ lb
garlic, slivered	2 cloves	2 cloves
salt and black pepper		
CRUST		
green pepper mustard	60 ml (4 tbsp)	4 tbsp
ground ginger	5 ml (1 tsp)	1 tsp
dried thyme	5 ml (1 tsp)	1 tsp
dried rosemary	5 ml (1 tsp)	1 tsp
roasted coriander (cilantro)	5 ml (1 tsp)	1 tsp
roasted caraway seeds	5 ml (1 tsp)	1 tsp
bay leaf	1	1
sea salt	2.5 ml (½ tsp)	½ tsp
vegetable oil	100 ml (3½ fl oz)	⅓ cup
GARLIC SAUCE		
garlic, unpeeled, but split into cloves	1 bulb	1 bulb
butter	45 ml (3 tbsp)	3 tbsp
ground black peppercorns	5 ml (1 tsp)	1 tsp
juniper berries	5 ml (1 tsp)	1 tsp
gin	15 ml (1 tbsp)	1 tbsp
chicken stock	100 ml (3½ fl oz)	½ cup
cream	250 ml (9 fl oz)	1 cup

Trim off excess fat from the lamb. Using a thin knife make a few incisions in the meat and stuff with slivers of garlic. Season lightly with salt and pepper.

To make the crust: Combine all the ingredients for the crust, spread over the lamb and stand for 1 hour.

Prepare an indirect fire and fit a foil drip pan between the coals. Place meat in a roast holder and position it on top of the grid over the drip pan. Cover the kettle and cook for 1½ hours. Stand for 5 minutes before carving and serving with the sauce.

To make the sauce: Blanch the garlic in water for 3 minutes, drain and peel. Sauté garlic in butter over a very low heat for 20 minutes, without allowing the garlic to discolour. Add the peppercorn and juniper berry mix, the gin and the stock and simmer for 5 minutes. Stir in the cream and bring to the boil. Purée and strain. Reheat and serve.

NOTE: The garlic sauce may be made in advance and reheated when required.

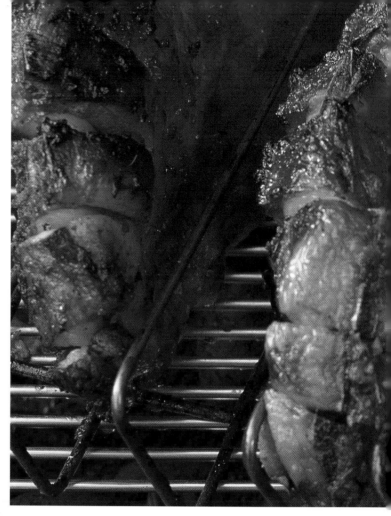

Kidney kebabs and Apple-flavoured lamb ribs

APPLE-FLAVOURED LAMB RIBS
(Serves 6-8 as an appetizer, 4 as a main course)

Indirect . . . 35 minutes. Rib rack

INGREDIENTS	METRIC/IMPERIAL	AMERICAN
lamb ribs or rib chops	2 kg (4½ lb)	4½ lb
canned apple sauce	400 ml (14 fl oz)	1¼ cups
chilli sauce	125 ml (4 fl oz)	½ cup
garlic, crushed	2 large cloves	2 large cloves
brown sugar	30 ml (2 tbsp)	2 tbsp
lemon juice	15 ml (1 tbsp)	1 tbsp
honey	30 ml (2 tbsp)	2 tbsp
Worcestershire sauce	15 ml (1 tbsp)	1 tbsp
chopped fresh rosemary leaves	10 ml (2 tsp)	2 tsp
salt to taste		

Combine all ingredients except lamb. Brush meat generously with mixture and stand for 1 hour.

Prepare an indirect fire, place a foil drip pan between the coals and position the meat on the grid over the drip pan, or place in a rib rack over the drip pan. Brush with

marinade, cover the kettle and cook for 25-35 minutes, basting and turning as needed.

SWEET AND SOUR LAMB RIBS

(Serves 4)

Indirect . . . 35 minutes

INGREDIENTS	METRIC/IMPERIAL	AMERICAN
lamb ribs or rib chops	2 kg (4½ lb)	4½ lb
orange juice	125 ml (4 fl oz)	½ cup
soy sauce	125 ml (4 fl oz)	½ cup
honey	125 g (4 oz)	⅓ cup
lemon juice	60 ml (4 tbsp)	4 tbsp
grated orange rind	30 ml (2 tbsp)	2 tbsp
garlic, crushed	1 clove	1 clove
ground ginger	5 ml (1 tsp)	1 tsp

Combine all ingredients except lamb, mixing well. Arrange lamb in a shallow pan, pour marinade over and refrigerate for at least 2 hours, or overnight.

Prepare an indirect fire and place a foil drip pan between the coals. Place meat on the grid over the drip pan. Cover the kettle and cook for 30-35 minutes, basting frequently and turning as needed, until meat is tender and a rich brown colour.

KIDNEY KEBABS (Serves 4)

Direct . . . about 8 minutes

These take very little time to cook, so serve them first to tease the taste buds.

INGREDIENTS	METRIC/IMPERIAL	AMERICAN
onions	8 baby	8 pearl
red wine	125 ml (4 fl oz)	½ cup
water	250 ml (9 fl oz)	1 cup
lambs' kidneys	12	12
vegetable oil	60 ml (4 tbsp)	4 tbsp
dried rosemary	5 ml (1 tsp)	1 tsp
salt	2.5 ml (½ tsp)	½ tsp
black pepper	pinch	pinch
melted butter or margarine	60 ml (4 tbsp)	4 tbsp

Parboil onions in red wine and water until almost cooked, about 10 minutes. Remove outer fat and membrane of kidneys. Cut kidneys three-quarters of the way through the middle and open out like a book. Remove centre core. Thread onions and kidneys onto separate skewers. Combine oil, rosemary, salt and pepper. Coat kidneys with the oil mixture. Roll onions in melted butter or margarine.

Prepare a direct fire and place skewers on the grid over glowing coals. Cook for about 5-8 minutes, until kidneys are cooked and onions golden.

CHOPS WITH MINT (Serves 6)

Indirect . . . 20 minutes

Loin chops are the best choice for this dish, and are delicious cooked this way and served plain or topped with garlic.

INGREDIENTS	METRIC/IMPERIAL	AMERICAN
lamb chops, 2.5-cm (1-in) thick	12	12
salt and black pepper		
vegetable oil	30 ml (2 tbsp)	2 tbsp
onion, sliced	1	1
chopped fresh mint	15 ml (1 tbsp)	1 tbsp

Season the chops lightly. Combine oil and onion slices and toss to coat. Add the mint. Top each chop with the onion mixture.

Prepare an indirect fire and fit a drip pan between the coals. Place the chops on the grid over the drip pan. Cover the kettle and cook for 20 minutes until a good brown colour.

HERB SMOKED SHOULDER OF LAMB (Serves 6)

Indirect . . . 1½ hours. Roast holder.

Shoulder of lamb is the sweetest, most succulent cut of lamb. Ask the butcher to bone it for you as it makes carving so much easier.

INGREDIENTS	METRIC/IMPERIAL	AMERICAN
boned shoulder of lamb	1.5 kg (3 lb)	3 lb
vegetable oil	15 ml (1 tbsp)	1 tbsp
salt and black pepper		
fresh rosemary, soaked	a few sprigs	a few sprigs
smoke chips (preferably hickory), soaked	30 ml (2 tbsp)	2 tbsp

Rub the meat with oil and season with salt and pepper. Prepare an indirect fire and fit a drip pan between the coals. Place the meat in a roast holder and put it on the grid over the drip pan. Cover the kettle and cook for 45 minutes. Sprinkle the damp rosemary and smoke chips on the coals, cover the kettle and cook for about 45 minutes more. Serve hot or cold with Spiced Peaches (page 91).

VARIATION

Slice 1-2 French loaves diagonally into 1.5-cm (½-in) thick slices. Spread one side of each slice generously with Fresh Pesto Mayonnaise (see below). Top with watercress or sunflower seed sprouts and add slices of cold smoked lamb. Drizzle with Coarse-grained Mustard Sauce (see below) and garnish with cherry tomatoes.

Fresh pesto mayonnaise: Fit the metal blade to the work bowl of a food processor and chop 75 g (2½ oz/¾ cup) fresh basil leaves. Add 3 egg yolks and 60 ml (4 tbsp) lemon juice and process for about 30 seconds. With the motor running, slowly pour 340 ml (12 fl oz/1⅓ cups) oil through the feed tube. Process until thick. Add salt and pepper and 60 ml (4 tbsp) lightly toasted pinenuts or almonds and process again. Store in the refrigerator for up to two weeks.

Coarse-grained mustard sauce: Blend together 125 ml oil (4 fl oz/½ cup), 100 ml (3½ fl oz/½ cup) coarse-grained mustard, 45 ml (3 tbsp) red wine vinegar, pinch cayenne, and salt and black pepper until thick. Refrigerate until required.

GREEK-STYLE LEG OF LAMB
(Serves 6)

Indirect . . . 1½ hours

INGREDIENTS	METRIC/IMPERIAL	AMERICAN
leg of lamb, boned	1-1½ kg (2¼-3 lb)	2¼-3 lb
garlic	1-2 cloves	1-2 cloves
salt and black pepper		
vegetable oil	15 ml (1 tbsp)	1 tbsp
lemon juice	30 ml (2 tbsp)	2 tbsp
fresh oregano	2-3 large sprigs	2-3 large sprigs
onions, sliced	2	2
tomato purée	60 ml (4 tbsp)	4 tbsp

Cut boned leg open and flatten the meat with a mallet to an even thickness. Make a few incisions in the lamb with a thin-bladed knife and insert slivers of garlic. Season lightly with salt and pepper and rub with oil. Brush with a little lemon juice and place oregano on top of the meat.

Prepare an indirect fire and place a foil drip pan between the coals. Add the onion to the drip pan. Place the grid over the fire and position the meat over the drip pan. Cover the kettle and cook for 1 hour. Remove drip pan from under the meat, pour off the excess fat, then place meat on top of the onions in this pan. Pour tomato purée over and any remaining lemon juice. Place drip pan with meat on the grid and cook, covered, for a further 20-30 minutes, depending on the size of the meat.

To serve: Slice thinly and serve in Pitta Bread (page 104) with a little of the gravy and Chopped Greek Salad (page 85).

Greek-style leg of lamb with Chopped Greek salad (page 85) in Pitta breads (page 104), Taramasalata (page 101) and Dolmades with lemon sauce (page 100)

LEG OF LAMB IN BUTTERMILK

(Serves 6-8)

Indirect . . . 1½ hours. Roast holder.

INGREDIENTS	METRIC/IMPERIAL	AMERICAN
leg of lamb	**1.5-2 kg (3-4½ lb)**	**3-4½ lb**
garlic, slivered	**1-2 cloves**	**1-2 cloves**
buttermilk	**500 ml (18 fl oz)**	**2¼ cups**
salt and black pepper		
fresh rosemary	**large sprig**	**large sprig**
butter, melted	**30 ml (2 tbsp)**	**2 tbsp**
lemon juice	**30 ml (2 tbsp)**	**2 tbsp**

Make a few incisions in the lamb and insert slivers of garlic. Place meat in a suitable container and pour buttermilk over. Stand for at least 6 hours, turning from time to time. Remove meat and pat dry with paper towel. Season lightly, top with a large sprig of rosemary and place meat in a roast holder.

Prepare an indirect fire and fit a foil drip pan between the coals. Place the meat on the grid above the drip pan. Cover the kettle and cook for 1¼ hours. Combine butter and lemon juice and brush lamb generously with this mixture. Cover and cook for a further 30 minutes, basting once more with lemon butter during this time. Stand meat for 5 minutes before carving. Serve with Pan-baked Potato Slices (page 76).

LOIN OF LAMB WITH BLUE CHEESE SAUCE **(Serves 8)**

Indirect . . . 45 minutes

INGREDIENTS	METRIC/IMPERIAL	AMERICAN
loins of lamb	**2**	**2**
salt and black pepper		
fresh thyme	**large sprigs**	**large sprigs**
BLUE CHEESE SAUCE		
butter	**60 g (2 oz)**	**¼ cup**
brandy	**75 ml (2½ fl oz)**	**⅓ cup**
Dijon mustard	**15 ml (1 tbsp)**	**1 tbsp**
blue cheese, crumbled or grated	**100 g (3½ oz)**	**¾ cup**
chicken stock	**100 ml (3½ fl oz)**	**½ cup**
cornflour (cornstarch)	**5 ml (1 tsp)**	**1 tsp**
cream	**100 ml (3½ fl oz)**	**½ cup**

Ask the butcher for 2 loins of lamb consisting of about 8 chops each. Ask him to cut through the vertebrae bones to make carving easier. Trim off any excess fat, season the meat lightly and top each loin with sprigs of fresh thyme.

Prepare an indirect fire and fit a drip pan between the coals. Place the meat on the grid over the drip pan, cover the kettle and cook for 45 minutes. Stand for 5 minutes before carving and serving with the sauce.

To make the sauce: Melt the butter in a shallow pan and when foaming add brandy and flambé. Now add mustard, cheese and stock and simmer until the cheese has melted. Combine cornflour and cream and add. Bring to the boil, stirring all the time. This sauce may be made in advance and can be reheated.

RACK OF LAMB WITH PESTO TOPPING **(Serves 8)**

Indirect . . . 1 hour

Serve this dish with or without the gravy.

INGREDIENTS	METRIC/IMPERIAL	AMERICAN
racks of lamb	**2×1.5 kg (3 lb)**	**2×3 lb**
salt and black pepper		
PESTO		
goats' milk cheese	**125 g (4 oz)**	**4 oz**
chopped fresh parsley	**60 ml (4 tbsp)**	**4 tbsp**
pinenuts or almonds	**60 ml (4 tbsp)**	**4 tbsp**
garlic	**1 clove**	**1 clove**
oil, preferably walnut	**60 ml (4 tbsp)**	**4 tbsp**
lemon juice	**30 ml (2 tbsp)**	**2 tbsp**
fresh breadcrumbs	**75 g (2½ oz)**	**1 cup**
GRAVY		
plain (cake) flour		
beef and chicken stock combined	**500 ml (18 fl oz)**	**2¼ cups**
gravy powder	**5 ml (1 tsp)**	**1 tsp**

Ask the butcher to cut between the vertebrae to make carving easier. Clean the ends of the rib bones by cutting and scrapping off the meat and fat.

Trim off any excess fat and remove the thin membrane that covers the meat, leaving only a very thin layer of fat. Season lightly.

To make the pesto: Process cheese, parsley, nuts and garlic until well blended. Add oil and lemon juice and process again, now add crumbs and process until combined. Spread over the prepared lamb.

Prepare an indirect fire and fit a drip pan between the coals. Place meat on the grid over the drip pan. Cover the kettle and cook for 45-60 minutes, depending on the thickness of the meat. Stand for 5 minutes before carving into serving portions.

To make the gravy: Place a little of the liquid and some of the crispy bits from the drip pan in a frying pan. Add enough flour to absorb the fat and cook until turning brown. Combine stock and gravy powder, add to the pan and bring to the boil, stirring all the time. Strain and serve with the meat.

COFFEE-GLAZED LEG OF LAMB
(Serves 8)

Indirect . . . about 1 hour 40 minutes

INGREDIENTS	METRIC/IMPERIAL	AMERICAN
leg of lamb	2 kg (4½ lb)	4½ lb
garlic, peeled and sliced	4 cloves	4 cloves
fresh rosemary	6 small sprigs	6 small sprigs
black pepper		
strong coffee	75 ml (2½ fl oz)	⅓ cup
butter, melted	75 g (2½ oz)	⅓ cup
lemon juice	10 ml (2 tsp)	2 tsp
grated lemon rind	5 ml (1 tsp)	1 tsp

Pat lamb dry and make small incisions in the meat with a sharp knife. Insert garlic and rosemary and rub the meat with pepper.

Prepare an indirect fire, place a foil drip pan between the coals and put the lamb on an oiled grid above the drip pan. Cover the kettle and cook for 30 minutes.

Meanwhile, combine coffee, butter, lemon juice and rind. Baste meat with the mixture and continue cooking, basting occasionally, until meat is done, about 25-30 minutes per 450 g (1 lb) in total cooking time. Stand for 15 minutes before carving.

SARATOGA CHOPS (Serves 4)

Indirect . . . 20 minutes. Shish kebab set.

INGREDIENTS	METRIC/IMPERIAL	AMERICAN
boned loin of lamb	1	1
salt and black pepper		
bacon	4 rashers	4 slices
chicken livers	8	8
onions, quartered	2	2
slices pineapple, quartered	4	4
MARINADE		
vegetable oil	45 ml (3 tbsp)	3 tbsp
soy sauce	15 ml (1 tbsp)	1 tbsp
dried thyme	5 ml (1 tsp)	1 tsp
red wine vinegar	30 ml (2 tbsp)	2 tbsp
bay leaf	1	1
brown sugar	5 ml (1 tsp)	1 tsp
chicken stock	60 ml (4 tbsp)	4 tbsp
tomato sauce	15 ml (1 tbsp)	1 tbsp

Sprinkle meat lightly with seasonings. Roll the meat up firmly and secure with poultry skewers (pins) at 2.5-cm (1-in) intervals. Cut through the meat in between each skewer. Remove the rind from the bacon and cut each rasher (slice) in half. Wrap bacon pieces around chicken livers. Thread onion, pineapple, chicken livers, then lamb onto a large skewer. Repeat.

To make the marinade: Combine all the ingredients, pour over the meat and stand for at least 30 minutes.

Prepare an indirect fire and fit a drip pan between the coals. Place the kebab either in a shish kebab holder or directly on the grid above the drip pan. Cover the kettle and cook for 20 minutes, brushing at least once with marinade. Serve on a bed of rice.

STUFFED LAMB DELUXE (Serves 6-8)

Indirect . . . 1 hour 40 minutes. Roast holder

INGREDIENTS	METRIC/IMPERIAL	AMERICAN
boned leg of lamb	1.5-2 kg (3-4½ lb)	3-4½ lb
STUFFING		
butter	45 g (1½ oz)	3 tbsp
mushrooms, finely chopped	200 g (7 oz)	2¾ cups
ham, finely chopped	150 g (5 oz)	1 cup
egg	1	1
garlic, crushed	1 clove	1 clove
cream	60 ml (4 tbsp)	4 tbsp
salt and black pepper		
fresh breadcrumbs	30 g (1 oz)	⅔ cup
SAUCE		
canned tomato soup	400 ml (14 fl oz)	1⅔ cups
beef stock	250 ml (9 fl oz)	1 cup
garlic, crushed	1 clove	1 clove
lemon juice	15 ml (1 tbsp)	1 tbsp
brown sugar	30 ml (2 tbsp)	2 tbsp
Worcestershire sauce	30 ml (2 tbsp)	2 tbsp
salt and black pepper		
red wine	60 ml (4 tbsp)	4 tbsp

First make the stuffing: Heat the butter and sauté the mushrooms. Cook over a high heat until most of the liquid has evaporated. Add remaining ingredients and stir to combine. Allow to cool before using. Lay the meat flat and fill with stuffing. Roll up and sew with thick crochet thread, then place the meat in a roast holder.

Prepare an indirect fire and fit a drip pan between the coals. Position the roast holder on the grid over the drip pan. Cover the kettle and cook for 1 hour.

Meanwhile make the sauce: Place all the ingredients in a saucepan and simmer for 15 minutes. Remove the meat from the roast holder and place it in a cast-iron casserole. Pour the sauce over the meat. Cover the casserole with a lid and position it over the drip pan. Cover the kettle and cook for at least 45 minutes, basting three times. Stand for 5 minutes before carving. Serve with the remaining sauce.

BARBECUED SADDLE OF LAMB
(Serves 10-12)

Indirect . . . 2¼ hours.

INGREDIENTS	METRIC/IMPERIAL	AMERICAN
saddle of lamb	5 kg (11 lb)	11 lb
garlic, slivered	5 cloves	5 cloves
vegetable oil	75 ml (2½ fl oz)	⅓ cup
rind and juice of a lemon		
salt and black pepper		
rosemary and oregano	few large sprigs	few large sprigs
butter	150 g (5 oz)	⅔ cup
lemon juice	100 ml (3½ fl oz)	½ cup
Coca-Cola	150 ml (5 fl oz)	⅔ cup

Using a knife, make a few thin incisions into the meat and insert slivers of garlic. Brush with a mixture of oil, lemon juice and rind. Sprinkle with salt and pepper and top with a few sprigs of herbs.

Prepare an indirect fire and fit a drip pan between the coals. Place the meat on the grid over the drip pan. Cover the kettle and cook for 1¼ hours. Bring the remaining ingredients to the boil and simmer for 5 minutes. Cool until syrupy. Brush the meat generously, then cover and cook for a further hour, brushing twice more. Stand for 10 minutes before carving.

CURRIED KEBABS   (Serves 6)

Indirect; Direct . . . 20 minutes. Shish kebab set

INGREDIENTS	METRIC/IMPERIAL	AMERICAN
boneless lamb (shoulder, thick rib or leg)	1.5 kg (3 lb)	3 lb
fatty pork	1 kg (2¼ lb)	2¼ lb
MARINADE		
vegetable oil	30 ml (2 tbsp)	2 tbsp
onions, sliced	3	3
curry powder	30 ml (2 tbsp)	2 tbsp
turmeric	5 ml (1 tsp)	1 tsp
chillies, finely chopped	1-2 small	1-2 small
bay leaves	2	2
ground ginger	5 ml (1 tsp)	1 tsp
whole coriander, crushed	5 ml (1 tsp)	1 tsp
smooth apricot jam	30 ml (2 tbsp)	2 tbsp
brown sugar	60 g (2 oz)	¼ cup
wine vinegar	150 ml (5 fl oz)	⅔ cup
water	300 ml (11 fl oz)	1¼ cups
cornflour (cornstarch)	10 ml (2 tsp)	2 tsp

First make the marinade: Heat the oil and fry the onions. Add curry powder, turmeric, chillies, bay leaves, ginger and coriander and fry gently for a few minutes. Add jam, sugar, vinegar and water and simmer for 10 minutes. Allow to cool. Cut the meat into 2.5-cm (1-in) cubes and thread onto skewers, two lamb to one pork. Place the skewers in a large shallow dish and pour the cold marinade over. Cover and leave at least overnight, turning from time to time.

Prepare an indirect fire and fit a drip pan between the coals. Arrange the kebabs either in a shish kebab holder or directly on the grid above the drip pan. Cover the kettle and cook for 15 minutes. Pull the kebabs directly over the coals and cook for a couple of minutes to give them the traditional black edges. Turn a few times. Stir the cornflour into the remaining marinade and bring to the boil. Serve with the kebabs, accompanied by plain or yellow rice.

STUFFED SHOULDER OF LAMB ITALIAN-STYLE   (Serves 6-8)

Indirect . . . 2 hours. Roast holder.

INGREDIENTS	METRIC/IMPERIAL	AMERICAN
boned shoulder of lamb	1	1
Italian olive oil		
freshly ground coarse salt and black pepper		
lemon juice	45 ml (3 tbsp)	3 tbsp
grated lemon rind	5 ml (1 tsp)	1 tsp
chopped fresh rosemary		
STUFFING		
vegetable oil	45 ml (3 tbsp)	3 tbsp
onion, chopped	1	1
garlic, crushed	2 cloves	2 cloves
spinach, blanched and chopped	about 300 g (11 oz)	about 1¾ cups
pork sausage meat	250 g (9 oz)	1 cup
brandy	45 ml (3 tbsp)	3 tbsp

Lay meat flat and brush both sides with olive oil. Sprinkle with salt, pepper, lemon juice, rind and chopped rosemary. Lay meat skin side down.

To make the stuffing: Heat the oil and sauté the onion and garlic for a few minutes. Add remaining ingredients and mix well. Lay the stuffing on the meat and roll up. Sew with thick crochet cotton, then place meat in a roast holder.

Prepare an indirect fire and fit a foil drip pan between the coals. Place the roast holder on the grid over the drip pan. Top the meat with a couple of sprigs of rosemary. Cover the kettle and cook for 1½-2 hours, depending on the size of the meat. Stand for 10 minutes before carving. Serve with Pan-baked Potato Slices (page 76).

Stuffed shoulder of lamb Italian-style, Pan-baked potato slices (page 76) and Chicken livers in red wine and rosemary (page 103)

GAME

G ame is prized for its rich flavours and textures but not many books supply recipes for cooking it on a barbecue kettle. Since it is as easy to cook as other meats we have included a few delicious ideas for venison, rabbit and guinea fowl. As venison tends to be dry, marinating it for at least 24 hours before cooking by the indirect method will ensure a meat that is tender and juicy and deep mahogany in colour.

Kettle-roasted rabbit (page 34), Roast guinea fowl (page 34), Roast fillet of venison (page 35)

ROAST GUINEA FOWL (Serves 4-6)

Indirect . . . 1 hour

INGREDIENTS	METRIC/IMPERIAL	AMERICAN
guinea fowl	2	2
onion, halved	1	1
apple, halved	1	1
fresh herbs	sprigs	sprigs
gin	30 ml (2 tbsp)	2 tbsp
vegetable oil	30 ml (2 tbsp)	2 tbsp
salt and black pepper		
bacon	6 rashers	6 slices

Place an onion and an apple half in each cavity. Add herbs and gin to this. Brush the birds with oil, season lightly and cover the breasts with bacon.

Prepare an indirect fire and fit a foil drip pan between the coals. Place the birds on the grid over the drip pan, cover the kettle and cook for 1 hour. Remove bacon and discard if too dry. Carve guinea fowl as for chicken and serve hot or cold.

KETTLE-ROASTED RABBIT WITH MUSTARD AND BRANDY SAUCE
(Serves 4-6)

Indirect . . . 1 hour 20 minutes

INGREDIENTS	METRIC/IMPERIAL	AMERICAN
whole rabbit, cut in half	2 kg (2¼ lb)	2¼ lb
coarse salt	5 ml (1 tsp)	1 tsp
whole coriander (cilantro)	7.5 ml (1½ tsp)	1½ tsp
dried thyme	5 ml (1 tsp)	1 tsp
black pepper	2.5 ml (½ tsp)	½ tsp
vegetable oil	30 ml (2 tbsp)	2 tbsp
streaky bacon	6-8 rashers	6-8 slices
onion, chopped	1	1
carrots, sliced	2	2
celery, chopped	3 sticks	3 stalks
white wine	350 ml (12½ fl oz)	1½ cups
Dijon mustard	7.5 ml (1½ tsp)	1½ tsp
dry mustard	7.5 ml (1½ tsp)	1½ tsp
cream	125 ml (4 fl oz)	½ cup
brandy	30 ml (2 tbsp)	2 tbsp
butter	5 ml (1 tsp)	1 tsp
plain (cake) flour	5 ml (1 tsp)	1 tsp

Pound the salt, coriander, thyme and black pepper until fine. Brush the rabbit with oil and then rub in the seasonings. Cover the rabbit with bacon rashers. Add the vegetables and half the wine in a shallow roasting tray or cast-iron casserole. Lay the rabbit sections on top of the vegetables.

Prepare an indirect fire and cover with the cooking grid. Place the roasting tray or casserole in the centre of the grid. Do not cover the rabbit. Cover the kettle and

cook for 1 hour 20 minutes, adding the remaining wine after half the cooking time. Remove the rabbit and carve. Keep warm.

To make the sauce: Bring the vegetables and liquid to the boil, either directly over the coals or on top of the stove. Add both mustards and cream and boil for about 5 minutes. Now add the brandy. Mix the butter and flour together and add to the sauce, bring to the boil, then strain and pour over the rabbit. Serve with baked or boiled potatoes.

VENISON KEBABS (Serves 8)

Indirect . . . 25 minutes. Shish kebab holder

INGREDIENTS	METRIC/IMPERIAL	AMERICAN
venison fillet or rump	500 g (18 oz)	18 oz
streaky bacon	8 rashers	8 slices
button mushrooms	16	16
onion	16 pieces	16 pieces
venison kidney or liver, cubed		
fresh rosemary	sprigs	sprigs
MARINADE		
onion, chopped	1	1
tomato purée	100 ml (3½ fl oz)	½ cup
tomato sauce	100 ml (3½ fl oz)	½ cup
honey	30 ml (2 tbsp)	2 tbsp
fruit chutney	30 ml (2 tbsp)	2 tbsp
salt and black pepper		
ground ginger	1 ml (¼ tsp)	¼ tsp
Worcestershire sauce	15 ml (1 tbsp)	1 tbsp
scorched and ground coriander (cilantro)*	10 ml (2 tsp)	2 tsp
vegetable oil	30 ml (2 tbsp)	2 tbsp
wine vinegar	60 ml (4 tbsp)	4 tbsp
dry mustard	5 ml (1 tsp)	1 tsp
curry paste	5 ml (1 tsp)	1 tsp

Cut the meat into 2-cm (¾-in) cubes and wrap each cube in a piece of bacon. Thread 8 skewers with meat, mushrooms, onion and either liver or kidney. Lay in a suitable dish.

Combine the marinade ingredients and pour over the meat. Stand for 4 hours, turning from time to time.

Prepare an indirect fire and fit a foil drip pan between the coals. Fit the kebabs onto the shish kebab holder and place over the drip pan. Top with a few sprigs of rosemary. Cover and cook for about 25 minutes. Place remaining marinade in a small cast-iron pot directly over the coals and allow to boil for at least 10 minutes. Serve the kebabs with rice and the boiled marinade.

* Spread whole coriander out on a baking sheet and bake in the oven at 160 °C (325 °F, gas 3) for 8 minutes. Remove and cool, then grind in pestle and mortar.

ROAST FILLET OF VENISON (Serves 6-8)

Indirect . . . 50 minutes. Roast holder

INGREDIENTS	METRIC/IMPERIAL	AMERICAN
fillet of venison	1	1
salt and black pepper		
bacon	6-8 rashers	6-8 slices
chestnut purée	45 ml (3 tbsp)	3 tbsp
sour cream	250 ml (9 fl oz)	1 cup
MARINADE		
red wine	200 ml (7 fl oz)	¾ cup
water	100 ml (3½ fl oz)	½ cup
onion, sliced	1	1
carrot, sliced	1	1
celery, sliced	1 stick	1 stalk
bay leaves	2	2
peppercorns	10	10
dried thyme	5 ml (1 tsp)	1 tsp
garlic	2 cloves	2 cloves
vegetable oil	60 ml (4 tbsp)	4 tbsp

Place the venison in a suitable container. Combine the ingredients for the marinade and pour over the meat. Stand for at least 24 hours, turning from time to time. Remove meat from marinade and pat dry with paper towel. Reserve marinade. Season meat lightly with salt and pepper, wrap the bacon around the meat and place in a roast holder.

Prepare an indirect fire and fit a foil drip pan between the coals. Place the grid in position and then stand the roast holder over the drip pan. Cover the kettle and cook for 40-50 minutes, until just cooked through. Stand for 5 minutes before carving. Serve with the sauce.

To make the sauce: Boil 250 ml (9 fl oz/1 cup) marinade until reduced by half. Add the chestnut purée and bring to the boil, then simmer for 5 minutes. Stir in the sour cream and bring to the boil. Just before serving reheat the sauce, adding any residue that may have collected in the drip pan. For a thicker sauce, thicken with a mixture of 5 ml (1 tsp) butter and 5 ml (1 tsp) plain (cake) flour.

VARIATION

Smoked venison fillet: Marinate the fillet as in the recipe above. Season lightly and then wrap in bacon. Cook the venison over an indirect fire for 20 minutes, then add 45 ml (3 tbsp) soaked smoke chips (preferably hickory) to each side of the fire. Continue cooking for a further 20 minutes. Allow to cool before slicing.

TO MAKE TAMARIND JUICE Soak 45 ml (3 tbsp) tamarind pulp with about 150 ml (5 fl oz/⅔ cup) warm water for 15 minutes. Strain off juice and discard pulp. The pulp may be purchased from Indian speciality stores.

BONED SHOULDER OF VENISON
(Serves 8)

Indirect . . . 2 hours. Roast holder

INGREDIENTS	METRIC/IMPERIAL	AMERICAN
shoulder of venison, boned	1 medium	1 medium
pork fat (spek)	250 g (9 oz)	9 oz
wine vinegar	150 ml (5 fl oz)	⅔ cup
salt	10 ml (2 tsp)	2 tsp
black pepper	2.5 ml (½ tsp)	½ tsp
ground ginger	2.5 ml (½ tsp)	½ tsp
STUFFING		
butter	60 g (2 oz)	¼ cup
mushrooms, finely chopped	200 g (7 oz)	2¾ cups
fresh rosemary	5 ml (1 tsp)	1 tsp
fresh breadcrumbs	30 g (1 oz)	½ cup
salt and black pepper		
cream	45 ml (3 tbsp)	3 tbsp
MARINADE		
onion, sliced	1	1
buttermilk	500 ml (18 fl oz)	2¼ cups
garlic	2 cloves	2 cloves
red wine	100 ml (3½ fl oz)	½ cup
SAUCE		
redcurrant jelly	60 ml (4 tbsp)	4 tbsp
sour cream	100 ml (3½ fl oz)	½ cup

Cut the pork fat into 6-mm (¼-in) thick strips. Lay these strips in a shallow dish and add the vinegar, salt, pepper and ginger and allow to stand for 1 hour.

Meanwhile make the stuffing: Heat the butter, add mushrooms and fry for 5 minutes. Remove from heat, add rosemary, crumbs, seasonings and cream. Lay the meat flat and stuff. Re-roll and stitch with crochet cotton. Using a larding needle, lard the meat with the pork fat. Place in a suitable container.

Combine the ingredients for the marinade and add to the meat. Stand overnight, turning from time to time. Remove meat from the marinade and pat dry. Place meat and a little marinade in a cooking bag.

Prepare an indirect fire and fit a foil drip pan between the coals. Place the cooking bag in a roast holder and position over the drip pan. Cover the kettle and cook for 25 minutes per 450 g (1 lb). Remove meat from the bag and stand for 5 minutes before carving. Serve with suitable vegetables and the sauce.

To make the sauce: Pour the residue out from the bag and into a saucepan, bring to the boil, add a little more of the marinade and simmer for 5 minutes. Now add redcurrant jelly and sour cream and simmer until the jelly has melted.

NOTE: With young venison the same recipe may be used but roast the meat in the roast holder without the cooking bag. Baste with extra marinade every 30 minutes.

PORK

From crisp chops to spicy ribs and succulent roasts, pork offers a wide variety of possibilities for the barbecue kettle. The rich taste of pork is enhanced by the smoky flavour, and the crackling on roasts is the best ever. Pork loin, fillets, ribs, chops, sausages, and baked hams are made tastier and more succulent with bastes, glazes and marinades. When cooked, pork should be creamy in colour and not pink; but take care not to overcook it as this lean meat tends to dry out.

Roast leg of pork (page 44), Chilli pepper cornbread (page 105) and Honey-glazed pork fillets (page 44)

GRILLED LEMON CHOPS   (Serves 8)

Direct; Indirect . . . about 30 minutes.

INGREDIENTS	METRIC/IMPERIAL	AMERICAN
pork chops, 2-cm		
(¾-in) thick	8	8
MARINADE		
lemon juice	45 ml (3 tbsp)	3 tbsp
dry white wine	45 ml (3 tbsp)	3 tbsp
chopped fresh thyme	15 ml (1 tbsp)	1 tbsp
vegetable oil	90 ml (3 fl oz)	⅓ cup
olive oil	30 ml (2 tbsp)	2 tbsp
salt and black pepper		

First make the marinade: Combine lemon juice, wine, thyme, both oils and plenty of black pepper. Add chops and turn to coat. Refrigerate for about 4 hours, turning meat several times.

Prepare an indirect fire and place a drip pan between the coals. Drain the chops and place on the grid directly over the coals to sear. Sprinkle with salt, turn chops over, basting frequently with the marinade and cooking for about 8 minutes in total. Position chops over the drip pan and cook, covered, turning once and brushing occasionally with marinade, for a further 20 minutes or until meat is cooked.

BARBECUED SPICY LOIN OF PORK

(Serves 6-8)

Indirect . . . 2 hours. Roast holder.

INGREDIENTS	METRIC/IMPERIAL	AMERICAN
boned and rolled		
loin of pork	1.5 kg (3 lb)	3 lb
Spicy Sauce		
(page 90)		
BASTING SAUCE		
rind and juice		
of 1 lemon		
water	200 ml (7 fl oz)	¾ cup
cider vinegar	200 ml (7 fl oz)	¾ cup
butter	45 g (1½ oz)	3 tbsp
Worcestershire		
sauce	15 ml (1 tbsp)	1 tbsp
dried sage	5 ml (1 tsp)	1 tsp
salt and black pepper		

Score the rind on the meat well, and then place meat in a roast holder.

To make the basting sauce: Combine all the ingredients in a saucepan, bring to the boil and simmer for 10 minutes.

Prepare an indirect fire and place a foil drip pan between the coals. Place meat on the grid over the drip pan, cover the kettle and cook the pork for about 2 hours, brushing with the basting sauce every 30 minutes.

To serve: Combine 200 ml (7 fl oz/¾ cup) of the remaining basting sauce with the Spicy Sauce and bring to the boil. Serve the pork sliced, with the sauce, baked potatoes and a green salad.

SPICY SAUSAGE   (Makes about 2.5 kg/5½ lb)

Indirect . . . 20-25 minutes.

INGREDIENTS	METRIC/IMPERIAL	AMERICAN
whole coriander		
(cilantro)	45 ml (3 tbsp)	3 tbsp
salt	20 ml (4 tsp)	4 tsp
black pepper	5 ml (1 tsp)	1 tsp
ground cloves	2.5 ml (½ tsp)	½ tsp
grated nutmeg	2.5 ml (½ tsp)	½ tsp
boneless pork	1.5 kg (3 lb)	3 lb
boneless beef	1.5 kg (3 lb)	3 lb
pork fat (spek)	450 g (1 lb)	1 lb
dried thyme	2.5 ml (½ tsp)	½ tsp
vinegar	150 ml (5 fl oz)	⅔ cup
sausage casings	3 m (10 ft)	10 ft

Spread coriander out on a baking sheet and bake in a 160 °C (325 °F, gas 3) oven for about 8 minutes. Remove and allow to cool. Grind coriander in a pestle and mortar and combine with salt, pepper, cloves and nutmeg. Cut meat into 5-cm (2-in) cubes, add the spices, then pass through a mincer (grinder). Cut the pork fat into tiny dice about 3-mm (⅛-in) square and add to meat together with thyme and vinegar. Using a sausage filler, fill the sausage casings. Refrigerate sausage for at least two days to allow the flavours to mature before cooking.

To cook: Prepare an indirect fire and fit a foil drip pan between the coals. Arrange the coil of sausage on the grid over the drip pan. Cover the kettle and cook for 20-25 minutes, turning the sausage after 15 minutes. The sausage remains moist and does not burn on the edges when cooked this way. Cut into pieces and serve with Traditional Barbecue Sauce (page 90).

NOTE: This sausage may be cooked from frozen in the same way, but allow 5-7 minutes extra cooking time.

COOKING SAUSAGES ON THE BARBECUE KETTLE Sausages may be cooked one of two ways, either as described in the recipe for Spicy Sausage or by preparing a direct fire and allowing the coals to burn down low. Place lightly pricked sausages on the oiled grid, cover the kettle and cook for 8-10 minutes, turning frequently.

Spicy sausage, Curried kebabs (page 30), Traditional barbecue sauce (page 90) and Polenta (page 79)

NASI GORENG (Serves 6-8)

Indirect . . . 15 minutes. Cooking (Manchurian) grill.

One of the best party dishes. Cooked on the Manchurian (cooking) grill, you can cater for about 15 people at a time. As these ingredients cook so quickly, your guests will all get piping hot, freshly cooked food.

INGREDIENTS	METRIC/IMPERIAL	AMERICAN
chopped celery	90 g (3 oz)	1 cup
chopped leeks	90 g (3 oz)	1 cup
chopped onions	90 g (3 oz)	1 cup
chopped parsley	125 ml (1½ oz)	½ cup
garlic, crushed	3 cloves	3 cloves
spring (green) onions, including green part, chopped	1 bunch	1 bunch
diced pork or chicken	500 g (18 oz)	3½ cups
peeled and deveined prawns (shrimps)	300 g (11 oz)	2½ cups
salt and black pepper		
soy sauce		
cold cooked rice	750 g (1½ lb)	4½ cups
vegetable oil		
sambal manis*		
sambal oelik*		
ham, diced	4 slices	4 slices
FRICADELLA		
minced (ground) meat	150 g (5 oz)	1½ cups
onion, chopped	½ small	½ small
salt and black pepper		
soy sauce	few drops	few drops
GARNISH		
two-egg omelette, cut into strips		
prawns (shrimps), cooked	8	8
chopped parsley		

Place all the vegetables into one bowl, the pork or chicken, prawns, seasonings and soy sauce into another and the rice into a third.

To make the fricadella: Combine all ingredients and form into very small balls. Fry briefly in a little hot oil.

Prepare an indirect fire and fit the cooking grill. Do not let the grill become too hot. Add 100 ml (3½ fl oz/½ cup) vegetable oil to the grill and when hot add a little sambal manis and a little sambal oelik. Now add the vegetables and the pork or chicken. Stir-fry for a few minutes, then add the rice and stir-fry until heated through. Add a little more soy sauce to give a good brown colour. Stir in the fricadella and ham.

To serve, pile onto a serving platter and top with a lattice of omelette strips. Garnish with prawns and parsley. Serve with fried eggs and a selection of the accompaniments that follow.

*Available at speciality stores.

ACCOMPANIMENTS

1. Lengths of fresh or pickled cucumber.
2. Pineapple rings fried in butter and sprinkled with red wine.
3. Chopped tomato and onion.
4. Fresh slices of banana or chunks fried in butter and sprinkled with coconut.
5. Combined toasted coconut and peanuts.
6. Krupuc: flaked crayfish, chicken or dried shrimps served with Peanut Sauce (page 90).
7. Shrimp slices or chips.
8. Chicken satay with Peanut Sauce (page 90): Thread small cubes of chicken onto thin skewers. Brush with soy sauce and grill.

PIQUANT PORK FILLETS (Serves 6-8)

Indirect . . . 20 minutes.

INGREDIENTS	METRIC/IMPERIAL	AMERICAN
pork fillets (tender loin)	3	3
vegetable oil	45 ml (3 tbsp)	3 tbsp
garlic, crushed	1 clove	1 clove
chopped fresh rosemary	5 ml (1 tsp)	1 tsp
dry marinade (page 109)	30 ml (2 tbsp)	2 tbsp
SAUCE		
beef stock	125 ml (4 fl oz)	½ cup
chicken stock	125 ml (4 fl oz)	½ cup
white wine	60 ml (4 tbsp)	4 tbsp
spring (green) onions, chopped	4	4
water	100 ml (3½ fl oz)	½ cup
Dijon mustard	10 ml (2 tsp)	2 tsp
cornflour (cornstarch)	7 ml (1½ tsp)	1½ tsp

Combine oil, garlic and rosemary and paint onto the meat. Sprinkle meat liberally with dry marinade and refrigerate for 3 hours.

Prepare an indirect fire and fit a foil drip pan between the coals. Place meat on the grid above the drip pan. Cover the kettle and cook for 15-20 minutes, until cooked through, but do not overcook.

To make the sauce: Combine the two stocks, wine and onions and simmer for about 20 minutes. Strain and return the liquid to the pan. Add water and any residue from the drip pan and bring to the boil. Combine mustard and cornflour, add to the liquid and boil until thickened.

Carve meat at a slight angle into 6-mm (½-in) thick slices and serve with the sauce.

Nasi goreng and Eastern pork sticks (page 103)

GLAZED GAMMON ROLL (Serves 8-10)

Indirect . . . about 2 hours. Roast holder.

INGREDIENTS	METRIC/IMPERIAL	AMERICAN
boned and glazed rolled gammon roll (ham butt) or gammon on the bone	1	1
ginger ale	1 litre (1¾ pints)	2 pints
onion	1	1
carrot	1	1
celery	1 stick	1 stalk
bay leaves	2	2
whole peppercorns	12	12
whole cloves		
SPICED PEACHES AND ORANGES		
canned peach halves	875 g (2 lb)	2 lb
oranges, peeled and sliced	2	2
sugar	150 g (5 oz)	⅔ cup
cider vinegar	125 ml (4 fl oz)	½ cup
stick cinnamon	2 small pieces	2 small pieces
whole cloves	3	3
GLAZE		
soft brown sugar	300 g (11 oz)	1½ cups
dry mustard	10 ml (2 tsp)	2 tsp
bourbon	100 ml (3½ fl oz)	½ cup

Soak the gammon for 6 hours in cold water, changing the water at least twice during this time. Place the gammon in a large saucepan, add ginger ale, vegetables, bay leaves and peppercorns. Bring to the boil and simmer until cooked, allowing about 20 minutes per 450 g (1 lb). (The best test is being able to lift off the skin easily.) Skim off any scum that collects and top up with water as the liquid evaporates. Remove the gammon from the liquid, draining well. Do not peel off the rind. Score the rind and fat in a diamond pattern and stud each diamond with a clove.

To make the spiced peaches and oranges: Drain the peaches and reserve the syrup. Place peaches and oranges in a bowl. Combine peach syrup with the remaining ingredients, bring to the boil and simmer for 10 minutes. Pour the hot syrup over the fruit, then cool, cover and refrigerate for 24 hours before serving.

To prepare the glaze: Combine all the ingredients in a small saucepan and warm slightly. Place gammon in a roast holder and brush generously with glaze.

Prepare an indirect fire and fit a drip pan between the coals. Place gammon on the grid over the drip pan, cover the kettle and cook for 15 minutes per 450 g (1 lb), brushing every 15 minutes with glaze. Stand for about 10 minutes before carving. Serve with the spiced-peaches and oranges.

NOTE: The gammon may be boiled the day before, then cooled and refrigerated. Complete the glazing when required.

Baked pork chops and Glazed gammon roll

BAKED PORK CHOPS (Serves 8)

Indirect . . . 25 minutes.

INGREDIENTS	METRIC/IMPERIAL	AMERICAN
pork loin chops, 2-cm (¾-in) thick	8	8
vegetable oil	30 ml (2 tbsp)	2 tbsp
salt and black pepper		
paprika	2.5 ml (½ tsp)	½ tsp
dry mustard	10 ml (2 tsp)	2 tsp
fresh sage leaves	16	16

Trim chops well and make three or four incisions in the pork fat to prevent the chop from buckling as it cooks. Brush very sparingly with oil and sprinkle with salt and pepper. Combine the paprika and mustard and rub into the flesh. Place two sage leaves on top of each chop.

Prepare an indirect fire and place a foil drip pan between the coals. Position the chops on the grid over the drip pan and cover the kettle. Cook for 20-25 minutes until a beautiful golden colour. Serve with apple sauce.

PORK CHOPS WITH
BARBECUE SAUCE (Serves 6-8)

Indirect; Direct . . . 20 minutes.

INGREDIENTS	METRIC/IMPERIAL	AMERICAN
pork loin chops, 1.5-2-cm/½-¾-in thick	8-10	8-10
vegetable oil	30 ml (2 tbsp)	2 tbsp
onions, chopped	2 medium	2 medium
chilli powder (American not hot)	15 ml (1 tbsp)	1 tbsp
orange juice	200 ml (7 fl oz)	¾ cup
tomato sauce	250 ml (9 fl oz)	1 cup
brown sugar	45 ml (3 tbsp)	3 tbsp
ground ginger	10 ml (2 tsp)	2 tsp
salt and black pepper		
dry mustard	5 ml (1 tsp)	1 tsp

Trim the chops well. Heat oil, add onion and fry until soft. Add chilli powder and orange juice and simmer rapidly until the orange juice reduces to a syrup. Add remaining ingredients. When cool, brush generously over the meat.

Prepare an indirect fire and place a foil drip pan between the coals. Position chops on the grid over the drip pan. Cover the kettle and cook for about 15 minutes. Brush with sauce once more, and then pull chops directly over the hot coals and cook with the lid off for 2-3 minutes on each side.

GRILLED SCHWEIN HACHSE
(Serves 4)

Indirect . . . 40 minutes.

INGREDIENTS	METRIC/IMPERIAL	AMERICAN
boiled ham hocks*	2	2
vegetable oil	45 ml (3 tbsp)	3 tbsp

Prepare an indirect fire and place a foil drip pan between the coals. Rub the skin surface of the meat with oil and place meat on the grid above the drip pan. Cover the kettle and cook for 30-40 minutes until the skin has become golden and crisp. Serve with Mustard Sauce (page 89), boiled potatoes and sauerkraut.

* Available from some German delicatessens or butchers. Also know as eisbein.

HONEY-GLAZED PORK FILLETS
(Serves 4-6)

Indirect . . . 25 minutes.

INGREDIENTS	METRIC/IMPERIAL	AMERICAN
pork fillets (tenderloins)	4	4
MARINADE		
honey	190 ml (6½ fl oz)	¾ cup
soy sauce	45 ml (3 tbsp)	3 tbsp
redcurrant jelly	45 ml (3 tbsp)	3 tbsp
grainy mustard	30 ml (2 tbsp)	2 tbsp
dry sherry	60 ml (4 tbsp)	4 tbsp
ground coriander	2.5 ml (½ tsp)	½ tsp

First make the marinade: Combine all the ingredients, mix well and bring to a simmer. Remove from heat and pour over meat. Marinate for 2 hours in the refrigerator.

Prepare an indirect fire and place a drip pan between the coals. Drain the fillets and position them on the grid over the drip pan. Brush with marinade, cover the kettle and cook for 20-25 minutes, brushing frequently with the marinade.

To serve: Carve pork diagonally into thin slices. Arrange on individual plates or a platter and spoon heated marinade over.

ROAST LEG OF PORK (Serves 12-16)

Indirect . . . 4 hours. Roast holder. Corn 'n' tater grill.

Ideal for feeding a large number of people; the meat is succulent and tender and the crackling as crisp as you'll ever find.

INGREDIENTS	METRIC/IMPERIAL	AMERICAN
leg of pork	4-5 kg (9-11 lb)	9-11 lb
salt and black pepper		
fresh sage leaves, chopped	about 60 ml (4 tbsp)	about 4 tbsp
vegetable oil	60 ml (4 tbsp)	4 tbsp
GARNISH		
apples	8	8
lemon juice	15 ml (1 tbsp)	1 tbsp
whole cloves	16	16

Score the skin of the pork well. Rub the meat all over with salt, pepper and sage. Brush lightly with oil. Place meat in the roast holder.

Prepare a large indirect fire. Place a foil drip pan between the coals and position the meat on the grid over the drip pan. Cover the kettle and cook according to the chart on page 109. About 30 minutes before the end of the cooking time, core the apples, sprinkle inside with lemon juice and cut each apple in half crosswise. Spike each half with a whole clove. Place apples on the corn 'n' tater grill, cover the kettle and allow to cook. Serve the apples with the meat.

OLD-FASHIONED BAKED HAM
(Serves 8-10)

Indirect . . . 1 hour

INGREDIENTS	METRIC/IMPERIAL	AMERICAN
whole cooked ham	2 kg (4½ lb)	4½ lb
whole cloves		
smooth apricot jam	225 g (8 oz)	¾ cup
redcurrant jelly	60 ml (4 tbsp)	4 tbsp
Dijon mustard	30 ml (2 tbsp)	2 tbsp
garlic, crushed	1 clove	1 clove
soy sauce	30 ml (2 tbsp)	2 tbsp
wine vinegar	15 ml (1 tbsp)	1 tbsp
pineapple juice	15 ml (1 tbsp)	1 tbsp
salt	pinch	pinch
smoke chips, soaked		

Score the fatty side of the ham in a diamond pattern and place a whole clove in each diamond. Combine jam, jelly, mustard, garlic, soy sauce, vinegar, pineapple juice and salt. Spread over ham and stand for 2 hours.

Prepare an indirect fire and place a foil drip pan between the coals. Add a handful of water-soaked smoke chips to the pan. Position the ham on the grid over the drip pan, cover the kettle and cook for 30 minutes with the vents half open. Remove cover, add more water-soaked smoke chips to the drip pan and, if necessary, add more coals to either side of the fire-bed. Cover the kettle and continue cooking for about 30 minutes more, adding 60 ml (4 tbsp) water to the drip pan if smoke stops coming through the vents.

SPECIAL BARBECUED RIBS
(Serves 8-10)

Indirect . . . 30 minutes. Rib rack.

Succulent and with a deep caramel colour, these ribs are a winner.

INGREDIENTS	METRIC/IMPERIAL	AMERICAN
well-trimmed ribs	8-10 portions	8-10 portions
mayonnaise	125 ml (4 fl oz)	½ cup
tomato sauce	125 ml (4 fl oz)	½ cup
prepared mild mustard	45 ml (3 tbsp)	3 tbsp
brown sugar	45 ml (3 tbsp)	3 tbsp
Worcestershire sauce	45 ml (3 tbsp)	3 tbsp
Tabasco sauce	few drops	few drops
soy sauce	45 ml (3 tbsp)	3 tbsp

Place the ribs in a large flat dish. Combine the remaining ingredients and pour over ribs. Allow to marinate for 6 hours, turning occasionally.

Prepare an indirect fire and place a foil drip pan between the coals. Place the ribs in a rib rack and position the rack on the grid over the drip pan. Cover the kettle and cook for 20-30 minutes, depending on the size and thickness of the ribs. Brush ribs at least twice during the cooking time with remaining marinade.

BARBECUED LOIN OF PORK
(Serves 10-12)

Indirect . . . 50-67 minutes

INGREDIENTS	METRIC/IMPERIAL	AMERICAN
boned loin of pork	1.5-2 kg (3-4½ lb)	3-4½ lb
salt and black pepper		
hamburger rolls	12	12
TOMATO SAUCE		
cider vinegar	190 ml (6½ fl oz)	¾ cup
tomato sauce	190 ml (6½ fl oz)	¾ cup
dried red pepper		
flakes	3 ml (½ tsp)	½ tsp
sugar	5 ml (1 tsp)	1 tsp
salt and black pepper		

First make the tomato sauce: Combine all ingredients except salt and pepper. Bring to a simmer, then remove from heat and season to taste with salt and pepper. Cool, then refrigerate until needed.

Rub loin of pork with salt and pepper, then tie into a good shape.

Prepare an indirect fire and place a foil drip pan between the coals. Position the pork on the grid over the drip pan. Cover the kettle and cook for about 17 minutes per 450 g (1 lb), basting with pan juices several times during the cooking time. Allow to stand for 10-15 minutes before serving.

To serve: Carve the meat very thinly, pile onto buttered hamburger rolls and top with the tasty sauce.

BAKED HAM **(Serves 12-16)**

Indirect . . . about 4 hours. Roast holder.

A wonderful way to prepare ham for Christmas. You'll be able to enjoy the holiday festivities with everyone else.

INGREDIENTS	METRIC/IMPERIAL	AMERICAN
leg of ham or		
pickled pork	1	1
GLAZE		
canned cranberry		
sauce, strained	400 ml (14 fl oz)	1⅔ cups
Crème de Cassis	125 ml (4 fl oz)	½ cup
soft brown sugar	200 g (7 oz)	1⅓ cup
ground cloves	1 ml (¼ tsp)	¼ tsp

Using a very sharp knife, cut through the rind from the shank bone to the base of the leg, then loosen, but do not remove, the skin all the way around the edge.

Prepare a large indirect fire and place a drip pan between the coals. Put the meat into a roast holder and

then on the grid. Cover the kettle and cook for 2-2½ hours. Now remove the skin and score the fat into a diamond pattern. Return the meat to the kettle for another hour.

Meanwhile, combine the ingredients for the glaze and heat slightly to combine. Brush the meat liberally with the glaze and cook for at least another hour, brushing with glaze every 15 minutes. Stand for 10 minutes before carving.

VARIATION
Add about 15 ml (1 tbsp) soaked smoke chips (preferably hickory) to each side of the fire during the last 30 minutes of cooking time.

SPICY PORK RIBS **(Serves 6)**

Direct . . . 15 minutes.

These are first baked in the oven, and then barbecued on the kettle until crisp and brown.

INGREDIENTS	METRIC/IMPERIAL	AMERICAN
pork ribs	2 kg (4½ lb)	4½ lb
garlic, chopped	2 cloves	2 cloves
dried chilli,		
crushed	1 small	1 small
ground coriander	2.5 ml (½ tsp)	½ tsp
ground cumin	2.5 ml (½ tsp)	½ tsp
aniseeds, crushed	2.5 ml (½ tsp)	½ tsp
salt	2.5 ml (½ tsp)	½ tsp
brown sugar	30 ml (2 tbsp)	2 tbsp
Worcestershire		
sauce	15 ml (1 tbsp)	1 tbsp
cider vinegar	250 ml (9 fl oz)	1 cup
tomato sauce	500 ml (18 fl oz)	2¼ cups
Tabasco sauce		
(optional)	few drops	few drops

Cut ribs into serving pieces and arrange in a single layer in a baking tin. Combine garlic, chilli, coriander, cumin, aniseeds, salt, brown sugar and Worcestershire sauce in a food processor and process until smooth. Place mixture in a saucepan and add vinegar and tomato sauce. Bring to the boil, then simmer, uncovered, for 30 minutes. If desired, add Tabasco sauce to taste. Pour sauce over ribs so that all portions are covered. Cover and bake for about 1½ hours at 160 °C (325 °F, gas 3). Ribs can be prepared to this stage and refrigerated for later use if desired.

To finish on the kettle: Prepare a direct fire and position the ribs on the grid over medium-hot coals. Cover the kettle and cook for 5-8 minutes, then turn ribs, brushing with more sauce if desired. Cook, covered, for a further 5-8 minutes until ribs are crusty and charred.

NOTE: If ribs have been refrigerated, stand at room temperature for about 30 minutes before placing in the kettle.

ROAST LOIN OF PORK WITH APPLE GLAZE (Serves 8)

Indirect . . . 1 hour 20 minutes-1 hour 40 minutes

INGREDIENTS	METRIC/IMPERIAL	AMERICAN
loin of pork,		
boned and tied	2-2½ kg (4½-5½ lb)	4½-5½ lb
apple juice	500 ml (18 fl oz)	2¼ cups
ground cinnamon	2.5 ml (½ tsp)	½ tsp
chilli powder	2.5 ml (½ tsp)	½ tsp
finely chopped		
onion	15 ml (1 tbsp)	1 tbsp
black pepper	1 ml (¼ tsp)	¼ tsp
salt	5 ml (1 tsp)	1 tsp
cornflour		
(cornstarch)	10 ml (2 tsp)	2 tsp

Place pork in a deep bowl. Combine all remaining ingredients, except the salt and cornflour, and pour over the meat. Cover and refrigerate for 4 hours.

Prepare a *large* indirect fire and place a foil drip pan between the coals. Lift pork from the marinade and drain. Reserve marinade. Score fat and rub with salt. Position the meat on the oiled grid over the drip pan, cover the kettle and cook for 18-20 minutes per 450 g (1 lb), brushing frequently with marinade during the last 40 minutes of cooking. Let the roast stand for 10-15 minutes before carving. Add cornflour to remaining marinade and heat, stirring, until slightly thickened. Serve with the meat.

ROAST SPICY LOIN OF PORK
(Serves 6-8)

Indirect . . . 2 hours. Roast holder.

INGREDIENTS	METRIC/IMPERIAL	AMERICAN
boned loin of pork	1.5-2 kg (3-4½ lb)	3-4½ lb
garlic, crushed	3 cloves	3 cloves
lemon rind	7.5 ml (1½ tsp)	1½ tsp
chopped fresh		
thyme	5 ml (1 tsp)	1 tsp
salt and black pepper		
vegetable oil	60 ml (4 tbsp)	4 tbsp
gin	15 ml (1 tbsp)	1 tbsp
brown sugar	10 ml (2 tsp)	2 tsp
tamarind juice		
(page 35)	250 ml (9 fl oz)	1 cup
bay leaves	2	2
soy sauce	15 ml (1 tbsp)	1 tbsp

Score the pork rind well, and then lay the loin flat, flesh side up. Combine garlic, lemon rind, thyme, salt and pepper, and rub onto flesh. Roll and tie meat firmly. Combine oil, gin and brown sugar and rub the mixture onto the surface of the pork. Place in a glass dish, pour tamarind liquid over, add bay leaves and soy sauce. Cover and refrigerate for 24 hours, turning occasionally.

Prepare an indirect fire and place a foil drip pan between the coals. Put the meat into the roast holder and position it on the grid over the drip pan. Cover the kettle and cook for 2 hours. Stand for 10 minutes before carving thinly.

GINGERED SPARERIBS (Serves 6)

Indirect . . . 45 minutes

INGREDIENTS	METRIC/IMPERIAL	AMERICAN
pork spareribs,		
parboiled*	3 kg (7 lb)	7 lb
GINGER SAUCE		
soy sauce	125 ml (4 fl oz)	½ cup
tomato sauce	125 ml (4 fl oz)	½ cup
chicken stock	60 ml (4 tbsp)	4 tbsp
brown sugar	45 ml (3 tbsp)	3 tbsp
grated fresh root		
ginger	30 ml (2 tbsp)	2 tbsp
HERB MIXTURE		
sugar	30 ml (2 tbsp)	2 tbsp
salt	2.5 ml (½ tsp)	½ tsp
paprika	2.5 ml (½ tsp)	½ tsp
turmeric	2.5 ml (½ tsp)	½ tsp
celery seed	2.5 ml (½ tsp)	½ tsp
dry mustard	pinch	pinch

First make the ginger sauce: Combine all ingredients for ginger sauce. Place spareribs in a large pan and pour sauce over. Cover and refrigerate overnight, turning once or twice. Remove spareribs from marinade and pat dry. Reserve marinade for grilling.

To make the herb mixture: Combine the ingredients and pat over spareribs.

Prepare an indirect fire and place a foil drip pan between the coals. Position spareribs on the grid over the drip pan and cook, covered, for 30-45 minutes, basting frequently with the ginger sauce. Separate into serving portions and serve with Chinese Plum Dipping Sauce (page 90).

TO PARBOIL RIBS Parboiling the spareribs before marinating and barbecuing will reduce the cooking time over the coals, resulting in spareribs that are juicy on the inside, crisp on the outside.

Place spareribs in a large saucepan and barely cover with cold water. Add 1 onion, quartered, 2 whole cloves, 1 bay leaf, 1 celery top, few sprigs thyme, 4 or 5 peppercorns, 3-cm (1¼-in) piece carrot and 30 ml (2 tbsp) lemon juice and bring to the boil. Reduce heat and simmer, covered, for 40-45 minutes. Drain and cool, then marinate as desired and barbecue as instructed.

PORK AND ORANGE KEBABS

(Serves 4)

Indirect . . . 20 minutes. Shish kebab set.

INGREDIENTS	METRIC/IMPERIAL	AMERICAN
pork fillets (tenderloins), cubed	2	2
oranges, segmented*	2-3	2-3
salt		
cherry (baby) tomatoes		
fresh basil	few sprigs	few sprigs
MARINADE		
frozen orange juice concentrate	100 ml (3½ fl oz)	½ cup
water	100 ml (3½ fl oz)	½ cup
honey	60 ml (4 tbsp)	4 tbsp
red wine vinegar	30 ml (2 tbsp)	2 tbsp
black pepper		
chopped fresh basil	15 ml (1 tbsp)	1 tbsp
vegetable oil	15 ml (1 tbsp)	1 tbsp
soy sauce	15 ml (1 tbsp)	1 tbsp

First make the marinade: Combine all the ingredients. Add the pork and allow to stand for at least 3 hours, turning from time to time. Thread meat and orange segments alternately onto thin wooden skewers. Sprinkle lightly with salt.

Prepare an indirect fire and fit a foil drip pan between the coals. Position skewers on the grid or in a shish kebab holder over the drip pan. Cover the kettle and cook for 10-15 minutes. Add 1 or 2 cherry tomatoes to each kebab and serve garnished with fresh basil on a bed of rice.

* Using a serrated knife, peel the orange and remove all the white pith. Cut into the orange, just to one side of each membrane, to release the segments.

SMOKED BACON (Makes 2 kg/4½ lb)

Indirect . . . 1 hour

Order the pickled pork belly a few days in advance from your butcher.

INGREDIENTS	METRIC/IMPERIAL	AMERICAN
strip of pickled pork belly	2 kg (4½ lb)	4½ lb
smoke chips (preferably hickory), soaked	about 30 ml (2 tbsp)	2 tbsp

Rinse the pork, pat dry and wrap in heavy-duty foil. Prepare an indirect fire and place a large foil drip pan between the coals. Position the meat on the grid over the drip pan. Cover the kettle and cook for 30 minutes. Sprinkle the soaked smoke chips on either side of the fire. Remove the foil from the meat and replace meat on grid. Cover the kettle and allow to smoke for 30 minutes. The rind will be a deep honey colour. Allow to cool, then wrap and store in the refrigerator. Slice thinly and cook as bacon.

CHINESE SPARERIBS (Serves 6)

Indirect . . . 40 minutes. Rib rack.

INGREDIENTS	METRIC/IMPERIAL	AMERICAN
spareribs, trimmed	2 kg (4½ lb)	4½ lb
soy sauce	90 ml (3 fl oz)	⅓ cup
honey	45 ml (3 tbsp)	3 tbsp
Hoi Sin sauce*	45 ml (3 tbsp)	3 tbsp
white vinegar	45 ml (3 tbsp)	3 tbsp
dry sherry	30 ml (2 tbsp)	2 tbsp
garlic	3 cloves	3 cloves
chicken stock	45 ml (3 tbsp)	3 tbsp
plum jam	200 ml (7 fl oz)	¾ cup
water	100 ml (3½ fl oz)	½ cup
cornflour (cornstarch)	20 ml (4 tsp)	4 tsp
TO SERVE		
celery curls		
Chow Faan rice (page 82)		

Lay the ribs in a large shallow dish. Combine the remaining ingredients, except the cornflour, and pour over the ribs. Allow to marinate for 6 hours, turning from time to time. Drain ribs, reserving the marinade, and slot into the rib rack.

Prepare an indirect fire and fit a foil drip pan between the coals. Pour 500 ml (18 fl oz/2¼ cups) boiling water into the drip pan. Position ribs on the grid over the drip pan, cover the kettle and cook for 30-40 minutes, depending on the size and thickness of the ribs.

To serve: Cut the ribs into serving portions, and garnish with celery curls. Blend cornflour into remaining marinade and bring to the boil. Simmer for a few minutes, then serve with the meat and Chow Faan Rice.

* Available at supermarkets.

POULTRY

Poultry is one of the most versatile items on the barbecue menu. A crisp, golden brown roast turkey, duck or chicken has great appeal, with tender, juicy flesh. Whether you are barbecuing chicken portions or whole birds, the results will certainly be tempting.

Poultry can be marinaded, smoked, glazed or casseroled on the barbecue kettle. Be sure to oil the grid before barbecuing any kind of poultry and make sure the grid is hot. These two tips will help prevent the meat from sticking to the grid.

Turn chicken portions in a sauce frequently to keep them from browning too quickly before the inside is cooked. To speed up the cooking of chicken portions, microwave them on 100% power for about 4 minutes before placing on the hot grid. Test whole roast birds to see if they are cooked by inserting a skewer into the thickest part of the meat, such as the thigh. If the juices run clear, the poultry is cooked. Whole birds need to stand for 10-15 minutes to firm up before carving.

Roast turkey with sherry butter glaze (page 57)

ORANGE AND CHUTNEY-GLAZED DUCK (Serves 4)

Indirect . . . 1 hour.

INGREDIENTS	METRIC/IMPERIAL	AMERICAN
duck	2 kg (4½ lb)	4½ lb
black pepper to taste		
GLAZE		
orange marmalade	300 g (11 oz)	1¼ cups
fruit chutney	125 ml (4 fl oz)	½ cup
brown sugar	60 ml (4 tbsp)	4 tbsp
cider vinegar	45 ml (3 tbsp)	3 tbsp
salt	10 ml (2 tsp)	2 tsp

Quarter the duck, trim off excess fat and skin and sprinkle lightly with pepper. Mix remaining ingredients together and set aside.

Prepare an indirect fire and place a foil drip pan between the coals. Position duck pieces on the grid over the drip pan, cover the kettle and roast for about 1 hour, turning pieces every 15 minutes. Brush duck generously with glaze during the last 10 minutes of roasting.

BARBECUED YOGHURT CHICKEN (Serves 4-6)

Indirect; Direct . . . 20 minutes

INGREDIENTS	METRIC/IMPERIAL	AMERICAN
chicken portions	1.5 kg (3 lb)	3 lb
chopped fresh coriander (cilantro)	15 ml (1 tbsp)	1 tbsp
MARINADE		
natural yoghurt	250 ml (9 fl oz)	1 cup
brown sugar	60 ml (4 tbsp)	4 tbsp
garlic, crushed	2 cloves	2 cloves
cider vinegar	45 ml (3 tbsp)	3 tbsp
Worcestershire sauce	10 ml (2 tsp)	2 tsp
Tabasco sauce		
salt and black pepper		

First make the marinade: Combine all the marinade ingredients in a blender or food processor.

Arrange chicken portions in a shallow dish and pour the marinade over. Cover and refrigerate overnight, turning from time to time. Drain chicken and pat dry.

Prepare an indirect fire and place a foil drip pan between the coals. Arrange chicken on the grid over the drip pan. Cover the kettle and cook for 15 minutes. Place chicken directly over the coals for about 5 minutes, basting with the marinade and turning as necessary. Serve garnished with coriander.

SPRING CHICKENS PORTUGUESE-STYLE (Serves 6)

Indirect . . . 45 minutes.

INGREDIENTS	METRIC/IMPERIAL	AMERICAN
spring (baby) chickens, split down the back	6 small	6 small
vegetable oil	200 ml (7 fl oz)	¾ cup
olive oil	45 ml (3 tbsp)	3 tbsp
garlic	3 cloves	3 cloves
salt and black pepper		
paprika	20 ml (4 tsp)	4 tsp
juice of a lemon		
bay leaves	3	3
cumin seeds	10 ml (2 tsp)	2 tsp
Portuguese chilli (peri-peri) oil to taste (page 91)		

Lay chickens, skin side down, in a large shallow pan. Blend all the remaining ingredients in a blender or a food processor until well combined. Pour mixture over the chickens and allow to marinate for at least 6 hours, turning from time to time. Lift chickens out of marinade and allow excess to drip off.

Prepare an indirect fire and place a foil drip pan between the coals. Arrange chickens on the grid over the drip pan, cover the kettle and cook for 45 minutes, basting with marinade at least twice during the cooking time and turning them over once. Heat any remaining marinade and serve with the chickens, baked potatoes and a green salad.

NOTE: If doing a large number of chickens, use the rib rack to hold them.

CHICKEN TERIYAKI (Serves 6-8)

Direct . . . 15 minutes. Cooking (Manchurian) grill.

INGREDIENTS	METRIC/IMPERIAL	AMERICAN
chicken thighs	20	20
vegetable oil	75 ml (2½ fl oz)	⅓ cup
MARINADE		
soy sauce, preferably dark Japanese	125 ml (4 fl oz)	½ cup
mirin*	90 ml (3 fl oz)	⅓ cup
sugar	30 ml (2 tbsp)	2 tbsp
ginger juice**	30 ml (2 tbsp)	2 tbsp

Firstly, remove the bones from thighs by making an incision down the length of the bone, towards the narrow end. Scrape the flesh away from the bone, then just pull the bone loose at the narrow end. Pierce the chicken skin to allow the marinade to penetrate and to prevent shrinkage during cooking.

Combine all the marinade ingredients, arrange chicken portions in a large shallow dish and sprinkle marinade over. Stand for 30 minutes.

Prepare a direct fire and heat the cooking grill. Add the oil, allow to heat. Drain chicken, reserving marinade, and pat dry. Fry chicken, skin side down, until brown, then turn the pieces over, cover the kettle and cook for about 10 minutes. Remove chicken, add marinade to cooking grill and bring to the boil. Add chicken, skin side down, cover the kettle and cook for a few minutes to give a good sheen. Slice chicken diagonally into 12-mm (½-in) pieces. Serve with Japanese or Basmati rice.

* Available at Japanese speciality shops and health shops.
** See page 52

ROAST GOOSE (Serves 6-8)

Indirect . . . 2½ hours. Roast holder.

INGREDIENTS	METRIC/IMPERIAL	AMERICAN
goose	3-4 kg (7-9 lb)	7-9 lb
butter	15 ml (1 tbsp)	1 tbsp
salt and black pepper		
STUFFING		
cubed crustless bread	90 g (3 oz)	3 cups
butter, melted	125 g (4 oz)	½ cup
Granny Smith apples, peeled, cored and cubed	2-3	2-3
stoned prunes, halved	125 g (4 oz)	1 cup
walnuts, chopped	60 g (2 oz)	¼ cup
salt	2.5 ml (½ tsp)	½ tsp
black pepper		
lemon juice	30 ml (2 tbsp)	2 tbsp
paprika	3 ml (½ tsp)	½ tsp
chopped fresh parsley	45 ml (3 tbsp)	3 tbsp
chopped fresh sage	10 ml (2 tsp)	2 tsp
APPLE SAUCE		
apples, peeled, cored and diced	3-4	3-4
water	60 ml (4 tbsp)	4 tbsp
salt	pinch	pinch
whole cloves	3	3
sugar	30 ml (2 tbsp)	2 tbsp
piece of lemon rind		

Rinse out goose cavity and pat dry. Lightly prick the skin with a fork. Spread butter over the breast and season well.

To make the stuffing: Combine all the ingredients and fill the cavity.

To make the sauce: Combine all the ingredients and simmer over low heat for about 10 minutes until soft. Remove cloves and lemon rind and purée.

Prepare a large indirect fire and place a foil drip pan between the coals. Position the goose on the grid over the drip pan. Cover the kettle and cook for 2-2½ hours. Serve with the apple sauce.

SMOKED CHICKEN WITH CURRY STUFFING (Serves 8)

Indirect . . . 2 hours

INGREDIENTS	METRIC/IMPERIAL	AMERICAN
chickens	2 whole	2 whole
onion, chopped	1	1
celery, chopped	3 sticks	3 stalks
curry powder	15 ml (1 tbsp)	1 tbsp
salt	5 ml (1 tsp)	1 tsp
black pepper	pinch	pinch
butter, melted	60 g (2 oz)	¼ cup
dried bread cubes	175 g (6 oz)	6 cups
apple juice	160 ml (5½ fl oz)	⅔ cup
smoke chips, soaked	175 g (6 oz)	3 cups
water		
extra apple juice		
vegetable oil		
SAUCE		
smooth apricot jam	250 g (9 oz)	1 cup
apple juice	45 ml (3 tbsp)	3 tbsp
brown sugar	30 ml (2 tbsp)	2 tbsp
chopped onion	45 ml (3 tbsp)	3 tbsp

Wash chickens and pat dry. Combine the onion, celery, curry powder, salt and pepper, butter and bread cubes. Moisten with apple juice and use to stuff the chickens. Tie legs and tail securely, fold neck skin under and twist wings behind back.

To make the sauce: Mix all ingredients together and heat gently to dissolve the sugar.

Soak the smoke chips in water, with a little apple juice added, for about 30 minutes.

Prepare a *large* indirect fire and when the fire is ready, add 500 ml (18 fl oz/2¼ cups) water and 250 ml (9 fl oz/ 1 cup) apple juice to the drip pan. Sprinkle half the soaked smoke chips over the coals. Place chickens on the oiled grid over the drip pan. Brush chickens with a little oil. Cover the kettle and cook for about 2 hours, or until chicken legs move easily in their sockets, brushing chickens with the sauce occasionally and adding more soaked smoke chips every 30 minutes. Add more water to the drip pan if necessary.

SMOKY CHICKEN WITH HERBS

(Serves 4-6)

Indirect . . . about 40 minutes

INGREDIENTS	METRIC/IMPERIAL	AMERICAN
chickens	2	2
lemon	1 large	1 large
chopped fresh		
tarragon	60 ml (4 tbsp)	4 tbsp
or dried	20 ml (4 tsp)	4 tsp
chopped fresh		
parsley	60 ml (4 tbsp)	4 tbsp
chopped fresh sage	10 ml (2 tsp)	2 tsp
or dried	2.5 ml (½ tsp)	½ tsp
garlic, finely		
crushed	1 small clove	1 small clove
vegetable oil	125 ml (4 fl oz)	½ cup
salt and pepper		
smoke chips, soaked		

Cut chickens into quarters. Trim off the backbones and flatten the breasts with the palm of your hand. Remove the last joint of the wings. Make several slits in the chicken legs.

Grate 5 ml (1 tsp) lemon rind and mix with the herbs. Squeeze the juice from the lemon and combine with garlic, oil and herb mixture. Rub the mixture into the chicken, pushing some into the slits in the legs. Cover and marinate for about 45 minutes.

To cook: Prepare an indirect fire and place a foil drip pan between the coals. Season the chicken with salt and pepper, then position the dark meat pieces over the drip pan. Cover the kettle and cook for about 20 minutes. Sprinkle a handful of soaked smoke chips onto the coals, add the chicken breasts, and cook, covered, for a further 15-25 minutes until pieces are crisp and tender. If necessary, baste the chicken with a little oil during this cooking time.

YAKITORI (Serves 4-6)

Direct . . . about 10 minutes

INGREDIENTS	METRIC/IMPERIAL	AMERICAN
boned and skinned		
chicken breasts	1 kg (2¼ lb)	2¼ lb
thin bamboo skewers		
Japanese soy sauce*	200 ml (7 fl oz)	¾ cup
sugar	75 g (2½ oz)	⅓ cup
sake**	45 ml (3 tbsp)	3 tbsp
GARNISH		
onion slices		

Cut the chicken lengthways into strips. Thread 1-2 strips onto each skewer. Bring the remaining ingredients to the boil and cook until reduced by half. Remove from the heat and cool.

Prepare a direct fire. Place the skewers on the grid and cook briefly on both sides. Dip into the sauce and cook again. Repeat this procedure three more times. Serve garnished with onion slices.

* Available from Japanese speciality shops.
** Japanese rice wine, available from off-licences (liquor or bottle stores).

CHICKEN STIR-FRY (Serves 6)

Direct . . . 10 minutes. Cooking (Manchurian) grill.

INGREDIENTS	METRIC/IMPERIAL	AMERICAN
chicken breasts,		
boned and skinned	4	4
vegetable oil	60 ml (4 tbsp)	4 tbsp
onion, sliced	1 large	1 large
French (green)		
beans, cut into 2-cm		
(¾-in) lengths	250 g (9 oz)	1½ cups
green pepper,		
chopped	1	1
carrots, sliced	2-3	2-3
mushrooms, sliced	200 g (7 oz)	2¾ cups
courgettes (baby		
marrows or		
zucchini), sliced	3	3
bean sprouts	150 g (5 oz)	2½ cups
sugarsnap peas	a few	a few
spring onions,		
including the green		
portion, chopped	6	6
garlic, crushed	1-2 cloves	1-2 cloves
red chillies, chopped	2-3	2-3
soy sauce	30 ml (2 tbsp)	2 tbsp
salt and black pepper		
ginger juice*	10 ml (2 tsp)	2 tsp
cashew nuts,		
coarsely chopped	100 g (3½ oz)	1 cup

Place chicken breasts in the freezer for 1-2 hours until very firm, but not frozen solid. Fit slicing plate to a food processor and slice chicken paper-thin.

Prepare a direct fire, fit a cooking grill to the kettle and allow to heat. Add the oil and, when hot, add the chicken. Fry for a few seconds, stirring continuously with a spatula. Now add all the vegetables, the garlic and chillies and stir continuously for 3-4 minutes. Add soy sauce, salt, pepper and ginger juice, stir to combine and continue cooking for a few minutes more. Serve in a shallow casserole, sprinkled with the nuts.

* **To make fresh ginger juice:** Grate fresh root ginger, squeeze pulp with your fingers to separate the juice from the pulp. Discard the fibrous remains.

Smoky chicken with herbs

GLAZED DUCK (Serves 3-4)

Indirect . . . 1½ hours. Roast holder.

INGREDIENTS	METRIC/IMPERIAL	AMERICAN
duck	2 kg (4½ lb)	4½ lb
onion	1	1
celery	2 sticks	2 stalks
butter	15 ml (1 tbsp)	1 tbsp
salt and black pepper		
ground ginger	2.5 ml (½ tsp)	½ tsp
GLAZE		
orange marmalade	275 g (10 oz)	1 cup
orange liqueur	60 ml (4 tbsp)	4 tbsp

Rinse out the cavity of the duck and pat dry. Cut the onion and celery in half and place inside the cavity. Spread butter on the breast and season with salt, pepper and ginger. Place duck in a roast holder.

Prepare an indirect fire and fit a foil drip pan between the coals. Position the duck on the grid over the drip pan. Cover the kettle and cook for 1¼-1½ hours.

Meanwhile make up the glaze: Heat the marmalade and liqueur until combined. Brush the duck with this mixture about three times during the last 30 minutes of the cooking time. Stand for 5 minutes before carving.

PEKING-STYLE DUCK (Serves 4)

Indirect . . . 2 hours. Roast holder.

INGREDIENTS	METRIC/IMPERIAL	AMERICAN
duck	2.5 kg (5½ lb)	5½ lb
boiling water		
salt	5 ml (1 tsp)	1 tsp
honey	60 ml (4 tbsp)	4 tbsp
red food colouring		
boiling water	125 ml (4 fl oz)	½ cup
spring (green) onions	2 bunches	2 bunches
Hoi Sin sauce*	250 ml (9 fl oz)	1 cup
Peking duck pancakes (page 104)		
ACCOMPANIMENTS		
shredded fresh ginger		
finely chopped fresh chilli		
light soy sauce		

Clean and rinse the duck, then hang in an airy place for 3-4 hours until the skin is dry. Place the duck in a colander with a roasting pan underneath and pour over about 1 litre (1¾ pints/4 cups) boiling water. Drain and pat dry. Combine salt, honey, red food colouring and the 125 ml (4 fl oz/½ cup) boiling water to make a syrup. Brush duck evenly with syrup and allow duck to dry for 1 hour. Coat the duck 2-3 times more until all the syrup has been used.

Prepare an indirect fire and fit a foil drip pan between the coals. Place the duck in a roast holder and then on the grid above the drip pan. Cover the kettle and cook for 1½-2 hours. If the duck begins to brown too early on in the cooking time, close the vents by about one-third. Open the vents again as the cooking process slows down.

To serve: Slice duck breast and remove dark meat from the bones. Serve with spring onions, Hoi Sin sauce, pancakes (page 104), ginger, chilli and soy sauce. Allow each person to place a few bits of duck flesh on a pancake, top with accompaniments, wrap the pancake around the filling and eat with the fingers.

* Available at supermarkets

GRILLED CHICKEN SALAD (Serves 4)

Indirect . . . 30 minutes.

INGREDIENTS	METRIC/IMPERIAL	AMERICAN
chicken thighs, skinned and boned	8	8
chopped fresh parsley	30 ml (2 tbsp)	2 tbsp
chopped fresh sage	10 ml (2 tsp)	2 tsp
butterhead (cabbage) lettuce	2 heads	2 heads
MARINADE		
vegetable oil	60 ml (4 tbsp)	4 tbsp
salt	5 ml (1 tsp)	1 tsp
coarsely ground black pepper	2.5 ml (½ tsp)	½ tsp
DRESSING		
minced (ground) pimiento (canned red pepper)	60 ml (4 tbsp)	4 tbsp
vegetable oil	60 ml (4 tbsp)	4 tbsp
white wine vinegar	30 ml (2 tbsp)	2 tbsp

First make the dressing: Combine all ingredients and season to taste with salt and pepper.

To prepare the chicken: Stuff the thighs with a mixture of parsley and sage, then flatten with the palm of your hand. Wash lettuce and pat dry.

To make the marinade: Combine the oil, salt and pepper and coat chicken with the mixture.

Prepare an indirect fire and place a foil drip pan between the coals. Position the chicken over the drip pan and baste with the marinade. Cover the kettle and cook for 25-30 minutes, or until done, basting frequently with the remaining marinade. Warm the dressing by placing it on the grid during the last few minutes of cooking time.

Cut chicken into thick slices and toss lettuce with warm dressing. Arrange lettuce on plates and top with chicken slices.

Peking-style duck with Peking duck pancakes (page 104)

ORIENTAL-STYLE TURKEY WITH NOODLE STUFFING (Serves 8-10)

Indirect . . . 2½-3 hours. Roast holder.

INGREDIENTS	METRIC/IMPERIAL	AMERICAN
turkey	4-5 kg (9-11 lb)	9-11 lb
melted butter	60 ml (4 tbsp)	4 tbsp
honey	30 ml (2 tbsp)	2 tbsp
soy sauce	30 ml (2 tbsp)	2 tbsp
NOODLE STUFFING		
Chinese egg noodles	250 g (9 oz)	1 package
salt and black pepper		
Chinese dried		
mushrooms*	6 large	6 large
vegetable oil	60 ml (4 tbsp)	4 tbsp
ginger juice**		
or grated fresh		
root ginger	10 ml (2 tsp)	2 tsp
soy sauce	45 ml (3 tbsp)	3 tbsp
sugar	5 ml (1 tsp)	1 tsp
dry sherry	10 ml (2 tsp)	2 tsp
cornflour		
(cornstarch)	10 ml (2 tsp)	2 tsp
water	125 ml (4 fl oz)	½ cup
garlic, crushed	2 small cloves	2 small cloves
pork sausage meat	250 g (9 oz)	1 cup
Hoi Sin sauce***	45 ml (3 tbsp)	3 tbsp
roasted peanuts	45 g (1½ oz)	⅓ cup
spring (green) onions,		
including green		
portion, chopped	60 ml (4 tbsp)	4 tbsp
canned red pimiento,		
diced	1	1
SAUCE		
smooth apricot or		
plum jam	60 ml (4 tbsp)	4 tbsp
soy sauce	60 ml (4 tbsp)	4 tbsp
Hoi Sin sauce***	90 ml (3 fl oz)	⅓ cup

Pour 2-3 litres (3½-5¼ pints) of boiling water over the turkey until the skin turns white. Pat dry and allow to dry in an airy place for about 5 hours – preferably hanging up.

To prepare the stuffing: Cook noodles in boiling salted water until just tender. Drain, turn into a large bowl and season well. Soak the mushrooms in a little cold water for 30 minutes, drain, then remove and discard the stems. Cut mushrooms into strips. Heat 30 ml (2 tbsp) of the oil, add mushrooms, ginger juice or grated fresh ginger, 15 ml (1 tbsp) soy sauce, sugar and dry sherry. Cover and simmer for 10 minutes. Mix 5 ml (1 tsp) of the cornflour with 60 ml (4 tbsp) of the water and add to the pan. Cook for 1 minute, then set aside. Now heat the remaining 30 ml (2 tbsp) oil, add garlic and sausage meat, and fry for about 3 minutes, stirring all the time. Add Hoi Sin sauce and remaining soy sauce and stir well. Mix remaining 5 ml (1 tsp) cornflour with remaining 60 ml (4 tbsp) water, add to sausage meat and cook until thickened. Add mushrooms and sausage meat to the noodles, along with the peanuts, spring onions and pimiento. Spoon the stuffing loosely into the front and rear cavities of the bird. Tie the legs together and secure the neck flap with poultry skewers (pins).

Brush the turkey with melted butter, season lightly, then place in a roast holder.

Prepare a large indirect fire and place a foil drip pan between the coals. Place the turkey on the grid over the drip pan. Cover the kettle and cook for 2-2½ hours. Combine honey and soy sauce, heating the mixture slightly if necessary. Brush turkey with this glaze, cook for 10 minutes more. Brush once again and cook for a further 10-15 minutes. Allow to stand for 10 minutes before carving and serving with the sauce.

To make the sauce: Combine jam, soy sauce and Hoi Sin sauce. Strain the liquid from the drip pan and add to the mixture. Heat, adding enough water to make a pouring sauce.

* Available in Chinese shops
** See page 52
*** This Chinese barbecue sauce is available at supermarkets

VARIATION
Smoked turkey To add a delicate smoked flavour, add about 60 ml (4 tbsp) soaked smoke chips (preferably hickory) to either side of the fire about halfway through the cooking time.

SPRING CHICKENS WITH SWEET AND SOUR SAUCE (Serves 4)

Indirect . . . 35 minutes.

INGREDIENTS	METRIC/IMPERIAL	AMERICAN
spring (baby)		
chickens	4	4
vegetable oil		
SAUCE		
vegetable oil	30 ml (2 tbsp)	2 tbsp
red wine vinegar	90 ml (3 fl oz)	⅓ cup
brown sugar	90 g (3 oz)	⅓ cup
orange juice	60 ml (4 tbsp)	4 tbsp
soy sauce	45 ml (3 tbsp)	3 tbsp
salt		
crushed aniseeds	2.5 ml (½ tsp)	½ tsp

Cut each spring chicken in half and pat dry with paper towels. Rub each half with a little oil.

For the sauce: Combine all the ingredients and set aside. Prepare an indirect fire and place a foil drip pan between the coals. Position chickens over the drip pan, cover the kettle and cook for 10 minutes. Brush chickens with the sauce. Continue cooking, covered, for a further 20-35 minutes, or until chickens are tender, brushing frequently with the sauce and turning as needed.

ROAST TURKEY (Serves 8-10)

Indirect . . . 2-3 hours. Roast holder.

INGREDIENTS	METRIC/IMPERIAL	AMERICAN
turkey	4-5 kg (9-11 lb)	9-11 lb
vegetable oil		
or butter	30 ml (2 tbsp)	2 tbsp
salt and black pepper		
WALNUT AND		
APRICOT STUFFING		
vegetable oil	100 ml (3½ fl oz)	½ cup
onion, chopped	1 large	1 large
turkey liver, chopped		
chopped fresh		
parsley	45 ml (3 tbsp)	3 tbsp
dried apricots,		
chopped	14	14
walnuts, chopped	100 g (3½ oz)	1 cup
eggs	2	2
dried thyme	5 ml (1 tsp)	1 tsp
dried tarragon	5 ml (1 tsp)	1 tsp
salt and black pepper		
fresh breadcrumbs	250 g (9 oz)	4 cups
SAUSAGE MEAT		
STUFFING		
butter	100 g (3½ oz)	⅓ cup
sausage meat	250 g (9 oz)	1 cup
garlic, crushed	1 clove	1 clove
dried tarragon	5 ml (1 tsp)	1 tsp
snipped chives	30 ml (2 tbsp)	2 tbsp
chopped fresh		
parsley	30 ml (2 tbsp)	2 tbsp
walnut oil (optional)	30 ml (2 tbsp)	2 tbsp
cream cheese	125 g (4 oz)	½ cup
salt and black pepper		

First make the walnut and apricot stuffing: Heat oil in a saucepan, fry onion and turkey liver for a few minutes. Combine with the remaining ingredients. Rinse out the turkey cavity and pat dry. Stuff the cavity with the stuffing.

Now make the sausage meat stuffing: Melt the butter and allow to cool slightly before combining with remaining ingredients. Using your fingers, loosen the skin of the neck cavity as far back as possible and stuff loosely to form a plump round breast. Stitch the flap onto the underside with cotton or secure with poultry skewers (pins). Tie the legs together with string if necessary. Rub the breast with oil or butter, season with salt and pepper, and then place in a roast holder.

Prepare a *large* indirect fire and fit a foil drip pan between the coals. Place the roast holder on the grid over the drip pan. Cover and roast for 2-2½ hours, depending on the size of the bird. Stand for 10 minutes before carving into serving portions.

VARIATION

Turkey may be cooked without stuffing: place a few whole onions, carrots and a bunch of fresh herbs in the cavity of the bird.

DUCK WITH OYSTER SAUCE
(Serves 3)

Indirect . . . 1½ hours. Roast holder.

INGREDIENTS	METRIC/IMPERIAL	AMERICAN
duck	2 kg (4½ lb)	4½ lb
onion	1 medium	1 medium
parsley	large sprig	large sprig
salt and black pepper		
vegetable oil	15 ml (1 tbsp)	1 tbsp
oyster-flavoured sauce*		

Rinse duck and pat dry. Cut the onion in half and place in the cavity of the duck with the parsley. Season the duck very lightly (the oyster sauce is salty), then brush with oil. Place duck in a roast holder.

Prepare an indirect fire and place an aluminium drip pan between the coals. Position the roast holder on the grid over the drip pan, cover the kettle and allow to cook for 1 hour. Remove the lid, brush duck liberally with oyster sauce, then cover and cook for 15 minutes. Brush duck with oyster sauce again and cook for a further 15 minutes. The duck will be golden brown and crispy. Serve as soon as possible.

* Available at major supermarkets.

ROAST TURKEY WITH SHERRY BUTTER GLAZE (Serves 10-12)

Indirect . . . about 2 hours. Roast holder.

INGREDIENTS	METRIC/IMPERIAL	AMERICAN
turkey, thawed	4 kg (9 lb)	9 lb
salt and pepper		
GLAZE		
butter, melted	250 g (9 oz)	1 cup
dry sherry	125 ml (4 fl oz)	½ cup
dried rosemary	2.5 ml (½ tsp)	½ tsp
dried sage	2.5 ml (½ tsp)	½ tsp
paprika	3 ml (½ tsp)	½ tsp

Rinse turkey and pat dry. Season cavity with salt and pepper. Bend wing tips under and tie legs.

To make the glaze: Combine the butter, sherry, herbs and paprika, mixing well.

Prepare a *large* indirect fire and place a foil drip pan between the coals. Place bird, breast side up, in a roast holder and position it on the grid over the drip pan. Cover the kettle and cook for about 15 minutes per 450 g (1 lb), brushing turkey frequently with the glaze during the last 45 minutes of cooking time.

NOTE: For stuffed turkey, increase the roasting time to 20 minutes per 450g (1 lb).

TANDOORI CHICKEN (Serves 6)

Indirect . . . 1½ hours. Roast holder.

INGREDIENTS	METRIC/IMPERIAL	AMERICAN
chicken	1½ kg (3 lb)	3 lb
natural yoghurt	150 ml (5 fl oz)	⅔ cup
lemon juice	45 ml (3 tbsp)	3 tbsp
fresh ginger juice*	5 ml (1 tsp)	1 tsp
garlic, crushed	1-2 cloves	1-2 cloves
chilli powder	1 ml (¼ tsp)	¼ tsp
vegetable oil	45 ml (3 tbsp)	3 tbsp
red food colouring	1 ml (¼ tsp)	¼ tsp
whole coriander, (cilantro) crushed	5 ml (1 tsp)	1 tsp
paprika	5 ml (1 tsp)	1 tsp
salt and black pepper		
ground fenugreek	2.5 ml (½ tsp)	½ tsp
garam masala	15 ml (1 tbsp)	1 tbsp

Make a number of incisions in the chicken skin. Combine all the remaining ingredients and spread this mixture all over the chicken. Cover and stand overnight in the refrigerator.

Prepare an indirect fire and fit a foil drip pan between the coals. Place the chicken in a roast holder and then on the grid over the drip pan. Cover the kettle and cook for 1½ hours, basting with some of the extra marinade three times during the cooking time.

* See page 52

CHICKEN WITH MUSTARD AND CREAM (Serves 6)

Indirect; Direct . . . 25 minutes

INGREDIENTS	METRIC/IMPERIAL	AMERICAN
chicken portions	12-16	12-16
butter	90 g (3 oz)	⅓ cup
rind and juice of an orange		
dry mustard	10 ml (2 tsp)	2 tsp
black pepper		
soy sauce	20 ml (4 tsp)	4 tsp
chicken stock	300 ml (11 fl oz)	1¼ cups
cornflour (cornstarch)	30 ml (2 tbsp)	2 tbsp
cream	75 ml (2½ fl oz)	⅓ cup
cress to garnish		

Arrange the chicken portions in a large shallow oven-proof casserole. Melt half the butter, add rind and juice of orange, mustard, pepper, soy sauce and half the stock. Pour over chicken and stand for 2 hours.

Prepare an indirect fire. Cover the chicken and bake for 15 minutes. Remove chicken portions from the casserole and arrange on the grid directly over the coals. Reserve the marinade. Melt remaining butter and brush over chicken. Grill, uncovered, turning as necessary, for about 10 minutes or until cooked through.

Meanwhile make the sauce: Bring the marinade to the boil, blend cornflour with remaining stock and add to the hot liquid, stirring until thickened. Add cream and reheat. Place chicken portions on a platter, pour a little of the sauce over and then garnish with cress. Serve the extra sauce separately.

ORIENTAL CHICKEN WINGS
(Serves 8)

Direct . . . 30 minutes

A dish for those who love hot spicy foods from the Far East.

INGREDIENTS	METRIC/IMPERIAL	AMERICAN
chicken wings	1 kg (2¼ lb)	2¼ lb
garlic	2-3 cloves	2-3 cloves
lemon	1	1
honey	15 ml (1 tbsp)	1 tbsp
soy sauce	125 ml (4 fl oz)	½ cup
chilli sauce	30 ml (2 tbsp)	2 tbsp
smoke chips, soaked		
DIPPING SAUCE		
dry wasabi powder*	30 ml (2 tbsp)	2 tbsp
lemon	½	½
soy sauce	125 ml (4 fl oz)	½ cup
vegetable oil	10 ml (2 tsp)	2 tsp
toasted sesame seeds	15 ml (1 tbsp)	1 tbsp

Remove last joint of each chicken wing. Finely crush the garlic and squeeze juice from the lemon. Mix garlic, lemon juice, honey, soy sauce and chilli sauce together and coat chicken with the mixture. Stand in the refrigerator for about 8 hours, or overnight, turning occasionally.

Meanwhile make the sauce: Mix wasabi powder with enough cold water to make a stiff paste, then allow to stand for 30 minutes. Squeeze the juice from the half lemon and combine with soy sauce and oil. Whisk in the wasabi paste to taste — be careful as it is very hot. Stir in the sesame seeds.

To cook: Prepare a direct fire and place chicken wings over medium coals. Cover the kettle and cook until beginning to brown and crisp, about 10 minutes. Turn with tongs. Sprinkle a handful of soaked smoke chips over the coals, then cover and continue cooking for 15-20 minutes until skin is crisp. Serve immediately with the dipping sauce.

* Wasabi powder is available from Oriental shops. Substitute with 5 ml (1 tsp) dried red pepper flakes and 2.5 ml (½ tsp) pure horseradish if necessary.

Tandoori chicken with sambals and Pilau rice (page 83)

ISLAND CHICKEN (Serves 4-6)

Direct . . . about 75 minutes.

INGREDIENTS	METRIC/IMPERIAL	AMERICAN
chickens, cut into serving portions	2	2
seasoned flour		
vegetable oil		
mayonnaise	250 ml (9 fl oz)	1 cup
chutney	190 ml (6½ fl oz)	¾ cup
pineapple juice	250 ml (9 fl oz)	1 cup
prepared grainy mustard	10 ml (2 tsp)	2 tsp
curry powder or to taste	15 ml (1 tbsp)	1 tbsp

Prepare a direct fire. Coat chicken portions with seasoned flour. Heat oil in a large cast-iron casserole over hot coals. Brown the chicken on both sides. Combine mayonnaise, chutney, pineapple juice, mustard, curry powder and mix well. Pour over the chicken and cover the casserole. Cover the kettle and cook for about 60 minutes, or until chicken is tender, stirring occasionally, and adding a little more pineapple juice if necessary.

SPATCHCOCKED TURKEY WITH GINGER-SOY GLAZE (Serves 10-12)

Indirect . . . about 1 hour 40 minutes

Spatchcock refers to a bird that has been split open and flattened for quicker, more even cooking.

INGREDIENTS	METRIC/IMPERIAL	AMERICAN
turkey, thawed	4 kg (9 lb)	9 lb
MARINADE		
vegetable oil	90 ml (3 fl oz)	⅓ cup
soy sauce	250 ml (9 fl oz)	1 cup
honey	100 g (3½ oz)	½ cup
red wine vinegar	45 ml (3 tbsp)	3 tbsp
grated fresh root ginger	10 ml (2 tsp)	2 tsp
garlic, crushed	2 cloves	2 cloves

First make the marinade: Combine all ingredients, mixing well.

Place turkey, breast side down, on a work surface. Cut down along one side of the backbone from neck to tail, cutting through the backbone and ribs. Repeat this process on the other side and pull the backbone free. Cut partly through the breast bone from the inside, then turn the bird breast side up with the drumsticks towards you. With a forceful motion, press down on the breastbone to flatten out the breast. Tuck wing tips under and tie legs together. Place turkey in a large flat container or plastic bag. Add marinade, coating the turkey well, and refrigerate for approximately 8 hours, turning occasionally.

Prepare a *large* indirect fire and place a foil drip pan in the centre. Position turkey, breast side up, in the centre of the grid over the drip pan. Cover the kettle and cook for about 12 minutes per 450 g (1 lb), basting often with the marinade during the last hour of the cooking time. Remove turkey from the kettle, stand for 15 minutes, then carve into serving portions.

CHICKEN JAMBALAYA (Serves 12)

Direct . . . 40 minutes.

Tasty to eat and fun to cook for a crowd. If you do not have a wok, use a very large cast-iron casserole.

INGREDIENTS	METRIC/IMPERIAL	AMERICAN
chicken thighs, boned	14	14
vegetable oil	75 ml (2½ fl oz)	⅓ cup
chorizo sausages *	750 g (1½ lb)	1½ lb
brown sugar	45 ml (3 tbsp)	3 tbsp
onions, chopped	4 large	4 large
celery, chopped	1 head	1 bunch
green peppers	2 large	2 large
garlic, crushed	3-4 cloves	3-4 cloves
chicken stock	1.5 litres (2¾ pints)	6 cups
salt and black pepper		
rice	700 g (25 oz)	2½ cups
cayenne pepper	1-2.5 ml (¼-½ tsp)	¼-½ tsp
paprika	40 ml (8 tsp)	8 tsp
spring (green) onions, including green part, chopped	3 bunches	3 bunches
tomatoes, peeled and chopped	3 large	3 large

Prepare a direct fire. Cut the chicken into smaller pieces. Fit a wok or use a large cast-iron casserole and heat the oil. Add chicken to oil and brown. Slice the sausage and fry with the chicken. Remove from the pan and set aside. Add brown sugar and fry until caramelized. Add onions, celery, green peppers and garlic and fry until tender. Return chicken and sausage to pan, add rice, stock, salt and pepper, cayenne pepper and paprika. Cover the kettle and cook for about 30 minutes, closing the top and bottom vents slightly to control the heat once the mixture has come to the boil and stirring twice during the cooking time. Add spring onions and tomatoes and stir in. Heat through for 5 minutes, then serve.

* This spicy Spanish sausage is available from some supermarkets and delicatessens.

Chicken jambalaya, Baked bananas with spice butter (page 97) and fresh oysters

FISH & SEAFOOD

The barbecue kettle is great for cooking fish, with results that are delicious, tender and juicy. The dry heat method allows fish to cook with little extra fat or oil for those who are diet-conscious, while the addition of butter or margarine, marinades and herbs enhances the flavour of lean fish.

Fish absorbs a slightly smoky flavour and cooks quickly. As it continues to cook after it is removed from the grid, take care not to overcook it. Delicate fish may fall apart easily when barbecued, so remember to oil the grid before placing the fish over the coals. For easy handling of fish fillets, try barbecuing them with the skin on. Use two flat spatulas or fish slices to turn the fish, and handle it as little as possible. The use of a hinged grill to hold delicate fish or small shellfish makes the turning easy.

Smoking imparts a subtle and delicious flavour to a variety of fish and is easily achieved in the barbecue kettle by sprinkling smoke chips over the hot coals.

Allow about 250 g (9 oz) per person; or 300 g (11 oz) for hungrier guests.

When purchasing fresh fish, look for clear eyes, shiny elastic skin, a clean, clear colour for white fillets, and a rich colour for dark-fleshed fish. Smell is a good indication of freshness - the fish should smell clean and fresh, just like the sea.

Portuguese-style prawns (page 72), Grilled sardines (page 68), Fish steaks with herbs (page 65)

In South Africa, fish and seafood cooked on the barbecue are gaining in popularity. With the many different varieties of fish available, it is often difficult to make a choice, but your fishmonger will be most helpful in recommending fish suitable for cooking on the barbecue kettle. The recipes in this chapter were devised and tested using particular fish and, therefore, we recommend yellowtail for Butterfly-Style Fish (below) and Blackened Fish (page 73), Cape salmon, steenbras or yellowtail for Fish Steaks with Herbs and Cape salmon for Marinated Salmon (page 72).

ROCK LOBSTER WITH HERB BRANDY BUTTER   (Serves 8)

Indirect . . . 15 minutes

INGREDIENTS	METRIC/IMPERIAL	AMERICAN
whole rock lobster	8	8
HERB BRANDY BUTTER		
butter	250 g (9 oz)	9 oz
garlic, crushed	2-3 cloves	2-3 cloves
chopped fresh dill	15 ml (1 tbsp)	1 tbsp
lemon juice	30 ml (2 tbsp)	2 tbsp
salt and black pepper		
brandy	60 ml (4 tbsp)	4 tbsp
chopped fresh parsley	45 ml (3 tbsp)	3 tbsp

Take each whole rock lobster and place it on its back, stretching out the tail. Using a sharp pair of scissors, snip away the entire membraneous undershell, leaving the head section intact. Make a 6-mm (½-in) deep cut down the centre of the exposed flesh to allow the sauce to soak in. Turn the rock lobster over and, using scissors, cut the centre of the back up to the head. Use the tip of the scissors to lift out the vein or alimentary canal that lies immediately below.

To make the butter: Combine all the ingredients and heat slightly to soften. At least 30 minutes before cooking, brush the flesh side of the rock lobster generously with the butter.

To cook: Prepare an indirect fire, place a foil drip pan between the coals and arrange the rock lobster, flesh side up, on the grid over the drip pan. Cover the kettle and cook for about 15 minutes, brushing once or twice during the cooking time. Serve immediately with a savoury rice mixture and a green salad.

VARIATION

Pistachio butter: Chop 60 ml (4 tbsp) shelled pistachio nuts in a food processor. Add 125 g (4 oz/½ cup) butter, 15 ml (1 tbsp) lemon juice, 2.5 ml (½ tsp) dry mustard, and salt and pepper. Process to combine, then shape into a roll, wrap in foil and chill well. Serve in slices or scoops with barbecued rock lobster.

Barbecued trout and Rock lobster with herb brandy butter

BUTTERFLY-STYLE FISH   (Serves 4)

Indirect . . . 25 minutes

INGREDIENTS	METRIC/IMPERIAL	AMERICAN
firm, white fish, butterfly-style*	1.5 kg (3 lb)	3 lb
lemon juice	30 ml (2 tbsp)	2 tbsp
salt and black pepper		
Italian olive oil	45 ml (3 tbsp)	3 tbsp
chopped fresh thyme	few sprigs	few sprigs

Pat the fish dry, then sprinkle both sides with lemon juice, seasonings, oil and thyme.

Prepare an indirect fire and fit a foil drip pan between the coals. Place the grid on top and position the fish over the drip pan. Cover the kettle and cook for 20-25 minutes. Serve with hot Lemon Parsley Butter Sauce (page 91).

*Ask your fishmonger to prepare the fish butterfly-style for you. This involves cutting off the head, cutting down the length of the belly and opening out the fish like a book.

FISH STEAKS WITH HERBS (SERVES 8)

Indirect . . . 15 minutes

INGREDIENTS	METRIC/IMPERIAL	AMERICAN
fish steaks	8	8
olive oil	75 ml (2½ fl oz)	⅓ cup
salt and black pepper		
coarsely grated rind of a lemon		
coarsely grated rind of an orange		
garlic	2-3 cloves	2-3 cloves
Dijon mustard	7.5 ml (1½ tsp)	1½ tsp
fresh basil or thyme chopped	8 sprigs	8 sprigs
chopped fresh parsley	30 g (1 oz)	⅓ cup
Feta cheese	250 g (9 oz)	9 oz

Pat the fish steaks dry, brush generously with the oil and then season lightly. Combine lemon and orange rinds, garlic, mustard and herbs and spread onto the fish steaks.

Prepare an indirect fire and place a drip pan between the coals. Lay the fish steaks on the grid over the drip pan, cover the kettle and cook for 10-15 minutes, depending on the size and thickness of the pieces of fish.

During the last 5 minutes of cooking time, top each piece of fish with cubes of Feta cheese. Serve immediately with new potatoes and a fresh mixed salad.

BARBECUED TROUT (Serves 6)

Indirect; Direct . . . 15 minutes

INGREDIENTS	METRIC/IMPERIAL	AMERICAN
trout, cleaned	6	6
salt and black pepper		
lemon juice	45 ml (3 tbsp)	3 tbsp
fresh dill or thyme	sprigs	sprigs
butter, melted	60 g (2 oz)	2 oz

Rinse the trout and pat dry. Season lightly, then sprinkle with lemon juice. Place a medium-sized sprig of fresh herbs in the cavity of each trout. Brush lightly with butter.

Prepare an indirect fire and place a foil drip pan between the coals. Position the trout on the grid over the drip pan, cover the kettle and cook for 10-15 minutes depending on the size of the trout. Brush the trout once again with butter, then turn them over so that they lie directly over the coals. Cook for a minute or two more just to 'singe' the skin. Serve immediately with Lemon Parsley Butter (page 91).

STIR-FRIED CALAMARI (Serves 6)

Direct . . . 4 minutes. Cooking (Manchurian) grill

INGREDIENTS	METRIC/IMPERIAL	AMERICAN
calamari (squid)	1.5 kg (3 lb)	3 lb
onions, chopped	2	2
garlic, crushed	4 cloves	4 cloves
fresh red chillies, finely chopped	3-4	3-4
vegetable oil	75 ml (2½ fl oz)	⅓ cup
finely chopped fresh root ginger	15 ml (1 tbsp)	1 tbsp
or ginger juice*	10 ml (2 tsp)	2 tsp
anchovy essence	45 ml (3 tbsp)	3 tbsp
water	45 ml (3 tbsp)	3 tbsp
dry sherry	60 ml (4 tbsp)	4 tbsp
oyster-flavoured sauce	60 ml (4 tbsp)	4 tbsp
salt and black pepper		
spring (green) onions, including the green portion, chopped	1 bunch	1 bunch
GARNISH		
chopped fresh coriander (cilantro)	45 ml (3 tbsp)	3 tbsp

Clean the calamari and cut into rings. Combine the onions, garlic and chillies.

Prepare a direct fire and when the coals are ready, place the cooking grill over the coals and allow to heat slightly. Add oil and heat. Stir in onion mixture and fry until soft. Add ginger and calamari and cook over a high heat, stirring all the time for about 2 minutes, until the fish becomes opaque. Add the remaining ingredients and stir-fry for a further 2 minutes. Transfer to a serving dish and sprinkle with coriander.

* See page 52

FISH IN NEWSPAPER (Serves 6)

Indirect . . . 45 minutes

INGREDIENTS	METRIC/IMPERIAL	AMERICAN
fish, head removed	2 kg (4½ lb)	4½ lb
salt and black pepper		
butter, melted	60 g (2 oz)	¼ cup
garlic, crushed	1 clove	1 clove
lemon juice	30 ml (2 tbsp)	2 tbsp
fresh thyme	5 ml (1 tsp)	1 tsp
spring (green) onion, chopped	1 bunch	1 bunch
chopped fresh parsley	45 ml (3 tbsp)	3 tbsp

Butterfly the fish from the belly side, remove the bone and season the fish lightly. Combine butter, garlic and lemon juice and drizzle generously onto the flesh sides of the fish. Sprinkle one side with thyme, spring onion and parsley, then sandwich the fish together. Wrap the fish in a sheet of greaseproof (wax) or parchment paper, folding it like a parcel. Wet 3 or 4 sheets of newspaper very well under running water. Wrap fish in wet newspaper.

Prepare an indirect fire and place a foil drip pan between the coals. Place the fish parcel in the centre of the grid, cover the kettle and cook for about 45 minutes. The newspaper will become very black, but inside the fish will be extremely moist, tender and full of flavour. Remove newspaper and greaseproof or parchment paper and serve immediately.

FISH BAKED IN SALT (Serves 6-8)

Indirect . . . 45 minutes

INGREDIENTS	METRIC/IMPERIAL	AMERICAN
whole fish, gutted but with scales	2.5-3 kg (5½-7 lb)	5½-7 lb
black pepper and mixed fresh herbs		
egg white	1	1
coarse salt	1 kg (2¼ lb)	2¼ lb
Lemon Parsley Butter (page 91) or Portuguese chilli sauce*		

Season the inside of the fish with pepper and herbs. Lightly beat the egg white, just to break it up, paint onto the fish and allow to dry slightly. Meantime grind salt to a slightly finer texture. Repaint fish and pack with salt. Allow to dry before turning over and repeating the painting and salting. Be very generous with the salt. Allow to dry for 15 minutes.

Prepare an indirect fire and place a foil drip pan between the coals. Place the fish on the grid, cover the kettle and cook for about 45 minutes.

To serve: Lift off the salt crust and skin and serve the fish off the bone, with a sauce of your choice.

* For Portuguese chilli (peri-peri) sauce, heat 250 g butter with 30 ml lemon juice and Portuguese chilli (peri-peri) oil (page 91) to taste.

Fish baked in salt and Fish in newspaper

FISH & SEAFOOD **67**

GRILLED SARDINES (Serves 4)

Indirect . . . 10 minutes

INGREDIENTS	METRIC/IMPERIAL	AMERICAN
sardines, thawed if frozen	8	8
vegetable oil	60 ml (4 tbsp)	4 tbsp
salt		
natural sesame seeds	250 ml (9 fl oz)	1 cup
SAUCE		
Worcestershire sauce	45 ml (3 tbsp)	3 tbsp
tomato sauce	45 ml (3 tbsp)	3 tbsp
dry mustard	2.5 ml (½ tsp)	½ tsp
lemon juice	15 ml (1 tbsp)	1 tbsp

To clean sardines: Slit the undersides of the sardines, up towards the tail. Cut through the backbone at the tail end, leaving the tail intact. Turn the sardines onto the belly side, and press with your thumbs to loosen the backbone, then carefully pull it out. Spread the fish flat, rinse well and pat dry.

Brush both sides of the sardines with a little oil and then sprinkle lightly with salt. Now coat the fish with sesame seeds.

Prepare an indirect fire and fit a foil drip pan between the coals. Arrange the fish in the centre of the grid over the drip pan, cover the kettle and cook for about 10 minutes. Serve immediately with the sauce.

To make the sauce: Combine all the ingredients and serve in small individual bowls. Dip bite-sized pieces of fish into the sauce.

PRAWN AND ONION KEBABS

(Serves 4)

Direct . . . 13 minutes

INGREDIENTS	METRIC/IMPERIAL	AMERICAN
prawns (shrimps)	16 medium	16 medium
baby (pearl) onions	16	16
courgettes (zucchini or baby marrow)	2	2
MARINADE		
garlic, finely crushed	1 clove	1 clove
chopped fresh oregano	15 ml (1 tbsp)	1 tbsp
or dried	5 ml (1 tsp)	1 tsp
vegetable oil	200 ml (7 fl oz)	¾ cup
dry sherry	45 ml (3 tbsp)	3 tbsp
salt and pepper		

Devein prawns but do not remove the shells. Slice open the prawns by about 1 cm (½ in). Parboil onions until almost cooked. Cut courgettes into 2-cm (¾-in) pieces.

Combine all ingredients for the marinade. Pour over the prawns, onions and courgettes. Marinate at room temperature for about one hour, or overnight in the refrigerator.

Thread prawns and onions alternately onto skewers. Place courgette pieces on separate skewers.

Prepare a direct fire. Brush kebabs with marinade and place over medium-low coals. Cover the kettle and cook for 5 minutes. Brush kebabs and turn. Cover and continue until cooked, about 4 minutes more for prawns and 6 minutes for courgettes.

BARBECUED LANGOUSTINES

(Serves 6-8)

Indirect; Direct . . . 10 minutes

INGREDIENTS	METRIC/IMPERIAL	AMERICAN
langoustines	2 kg (4½ lb)	4½ lb
HERB SAUCE		
chopped fresh parsley	45 ml (3 tbsp)	3 tbsp
garlic, crushed	3-4 cloves	3-4 cloves
chopped fresh thyme	10 ml (2 tsp)	2 tsp
chopped fresh tarragon	20 ml (4 tsp)	4 tsp
butter	400 g (14 oz)	1¾ cups
vegetable oil	200 ml (7 fl oz)	¾ cup
lemon juice	60 ml (4 tbsp)	4 tbsp
paprika	20 ml (4 tsp)	4 tsp
salt and black pepper		
dry mustard	5 ml (1 tsp)	1 tsp
cayenne pepper		
Worcestershire sauce	10 ml (2 tsp)	2 tsp

To prepare the langoustine: Take each whole langoustine and place it on its back, stretching out the tail. Now with a pair of pointed scissors snip away the entire membraneous undershell, leaving the head section intact. Make a 6-mm (¼-in) cut down the centre of the exposed flesh to allow the sauce to soak in. Turn the langoustine over and, using scissors, cut along the centre of the back up to the head. Lift out the alimentary canal that lies immediately below.

To make the herb sauce: Place all the ingredients in the work bowl of a food processor and pulse to combine. Place in a small saucepan over a very low heat until the butter has just melted. Using a brush, coat the flesh generously with sauce and allow to stand for at least 1 hour. Brush once more with sauce.

Prepare an indirect fire, fit a foil drip pan between the coals and then place the grid on top. Lay the langoustines over the drip pan, cover the kettle and cook for 6-8 minutes. Pull the langoustines directly over the coals for a further 2-3 minutes, just to char the edges. Heat the remaining sauce until piping hot and serve separately with savoury rice.

SMOKED ANGELFISH (Serves 3-4)

Indirect . . . 20 minutes

INGREDIENTS	METRIC/IMPERIAL	AMERICAN
angelfish	1 kg (2¼ lb)	2¼ lb
salt and black pepper		
turmeric	pinch	pinch
cayenne pepper	pinch	pinch
smoke chips	30 g (1 oz)	½ cup

Sprinkle fish with salt, pepper, turmeric and cayenne. Prepare an indirect fire and fit a foil drip pan between the coals. Soak the smoke chips in water for 10 minutes, then add to the coals. Lay the fish on the grid over the drip pan. Cover the kettle and cook for about 20 minutes. Allow to cool before serving.

VARIATION

Smoked pike (snoek): Use a cleaned and boned (skin still on) 1½ kg (3 lb) pike (snoek). Fold over as though the bone is still in the middle. Season with salt, black pepper, turmeric and cayenne pepper. Cook as above for 20-30 minutes depending on the thickness of the fish.

SMOKED TROUT (Serves 6)

Indirect . . . 15 minutes

Serve freshly smoked trout with crusty wholemeal (wholewheat) bread and a well-chilled, crisp white wine. Smoking brings out the best in trout — the flesh is moist with a subtle flavour.

INGREDIENTS	METRIC/IMPERIAL	AMERICAN
trout, cleaned	6	6
lemon juice	45 ml (3 tbsp)	3 tbsp
salt and black pepper		
paprika		
fresh thyme or		
lemon thyme	sprigs	sprigs
smoke chips, soaked	30 ml (2 tbsp)	2 tbsp
butterhead (cabbage)		
lettuce leaves		
apples, cored and cut		
into thin wedges	1-2	1-2
cress		
HORSERADISH AND		
APPLE SAUCE		
sour cream	250 ml (9 fl oz)	1 cup
Granny Smith (hard		
green) apple, diced	1	1
freshly grated		
horseradish	25 ml (5 tsp)	5 tsp
lemon juice	15 ml (1 tbsp)	1 tbsp
salt and black pepper		

Sprinkle the trout with lemon juice and then with salt, pepper and paprika. Place a medium-sized sprig of herbs inside each trout.

Prepare an indirect fire and place a foil drip pan between the coals. Arrange trout on the grid over the drip pan. Sprinkle the smoke chips over the hot coals, cover the kettle and cook for 10-15 minutes, depending on the size of the trout. Remove trout and allow to cool slightly. Serve either warm or cold.

To make the sauce: Combine all the ingredients, stand for at least 15 minutes to allow the flavours to develop before serving.

To serve: Cut the skin along the spine of the fish and across the head. Now role the skin down towards the tail. The skin may either be removed totally or it may be left in a roll at the tail. Serve each trout on a lettuce leaf with 2-3 apple wedges, a serving of sauce and a few sprigs of cress.

TROUT IN BACON (Serves 8)

Direct . . . 11 minutes

INGREDIENTS	METRIC/IMPERIAL	AMERICAN
trout, cleaned, with		
heads and tails		
intact	8 × 250 g (9 oz)	8 × 9 oz
salt and pepper		
to taste		
bacon, crisply		
cooked	8 rashers	8 slices
bacon, partly cooked,		
rinds removed	about 16 rashers	about 16 slices
MARINADE		
vegetable oil	250 ml (9 fl oz)	1 cup
fresh lemon juice	60 ml (4 tbsp)	4 tbsp
grated lemon rind	5 ml (1 tsp)	1 tsp
chopped fresh dill	10 ml (2 tsp)	2 tsp
GARNISH		
lemon wedges		

First make the marinade: Combine oil, lemon juice, lemon rind and dill in a large plastic bag. Add fish and toss bag to coat fish. Allow to stand for 1 hour. Remove fish and shake off excess marinade. Season insides of fish well with salt and pepper. Place one crisp bacon rasher (slice) in each fish. Wrap each fish in the partly cooked bacon, securing with wooden cocktail sticks (toothpicks).

Prepare a direct fire and oil the grid. Place fish on the grid, cover the kettle and cook for 5-6 minutes. Turn fish and cook, covered, for another 5 minutes, or until fish flakes easily with a fork and the bacon is crisp. Serve fish garnished with lemon wedges.

PAELLA (Serves 8)

Direct . . . 1 hour

INGREDIENTS	METRIC/IMPERIAL	AMERICAN
olive oil	90 ml (3 fl oz)	⅓ cup
chicken, jointed	1	1
salt and black pepper		
boneless pork,		
cubed	100 g (3½ oz)	¾ cup
chorizo sausages*	4	4
onions, chopped	2	2
garlic, crushed	2 cloves	2 cloves
green or red pepper,		
cut in julienned		
strips	1	1
tomatoes, peeled		
and chopped	2	2
boiling water	1.2 litres (2¼ pints)	5 cups
rice	400 g (14 oz)	2 cups
salt	3 ml (½ tsp)	½ tsp
chicken stock cube,		
crumbled	1	1
or chicken stock		
powder	10 ml (2 tsp)	2 tsp
saffron	8 threads	8 threads
calamari (squid),		
cleaned and cut		
into rings	2	2
firm white fish,		
cleaned	1 small	1 small
prawns (shrimps),		
veins removed	8	8
rock lobster tails,		
cut lengthways		
into four	2	2
fresh clams	8	8
fresh mussels	8	8
frozen peas	100 g (3½ oz)	½ cup
black olives	60 g (2 oz)	⅓ cup
lemons, cut into		
wedges	2	2

Prepare a direct fire and fit a wok or place a large paella pan onto the grid. Heat 45 ml (3 tbsp) of the olive oil until a haze begins to form. Season the chicken portions, add to the pan and brown well. Remove chicken, drain and set aside. Add the remaining oil to the pan, add pork and sausages and fry for a minute or two, then remove and set aside. Now add onions, garlic, green or red pepper and tomato. Cook for about 5 minutes, stirring all the time to prevent the ingredients from browning. Add boiling water, rice, salt, chicken stock cube or powder, and saffron, and stir to combine. Arrange chicken on top. Cover the kettle and cook for 15 minutes. Remove the lid, stir the mixture, then add the pork, sausages, calamari, white fish, prawns, rock lobster, clams, mussels and peas. Cover the kettle and cook until most of the liquid has evaporated and the rice has softened, about 20 minutes. Break line-fish into pieces using two forks.

To serve: Top paella with olives and lemon wedges and serve piping hot.

* A rich garlic-flavoured spicy pork sausage available from delicatessens.

MARINATED CALAMARI
(Serves 6)

Direct . . . 5 minutes

Calamari (squid) is simple to prepare and cooks almost instantly and has a special flavour when cooked over the coals. Three unusual and tasty marinades follow. Try them all!

INGREDIENTS	METRIC/IMPERIAL	AMERICAN
calamari (squid)	4-5 large	4-5 large
JAPANESE MARINADE		
soy sauce	150 ml (5 fl oz)	⅔ cup
Japanese sake*	150 ml (5 fl oz)	⅔ cup
mirin**	150 ml (5 fl oz)	⅔ cup
CHINESE MARINADE		
fresh ginger juice	5 ml (1 tsp)	1 tsp
sugar	10 ml (2 tsp)	2 tsp
anchovy essence	10 ml (2 tsp)	2 tsp
weak chicken stock	100 ml (3½ fl oz)	½ cup
ITALIAN MARINADE		
Italian olive oil	45 ml (3 tbsp)	3 tbsp
lemon juice	30 ml (2 tbsp)	2 tbsp
salt and black pepper		
dried thyme	2.5 ml (½ tsp)	½ tsp
soy sauce	15 ml (1 tbsp)	1 tbsp

To clean calamari: Remove the skin and pull out the 'plastic' spine. Rinse well and cut in half or quarters lengthways. Pat dry.

Combine all the ingredients for the marinade of your choice in a non-metallic pan. Add calamari and marinate for at least 3 hours.

Prepare a direct fire, arrange calamari over the coals and cook, uncovered, for about 5 minutes, turning the calamari halfway through the cooking time, and brushing once or twice with the marinade. Remember that calamari toughens when cooked for too long. Serve garnished with lemon wedges and sprigs of fresh herbs.

NOTE: To prevent the calamari from curling, thread onto thin wooden skewers that have been soaked in water for 15 minutes.

* Available from off-licences (liquor or bottle stores).
** Available from Japanese speciality shops.

Paella

POACHED FISH WITH FENNEL
(Serves 4)

Indirect . . . 25 minutes

INGREDIENTS	METRIC/IMPERIAL	AMERICAN
red snappers, cleaned	2 × 750 g (1½ lb)	2 × 1½ lb
STUFFING		
butter	30 g (1 oz)	2 tbsp
onion, chopped	1	1
large fennel bulbs, chopped	2	2
chopped chives	15 ml (1 tbsp)	1 tbsp
smoked ham, chopped	60 g (2 oz)	¼ cup
chopped fresh parsley	30 ml (2 tbsp)	2 tbsp
Pernod	10 ml (2 tsp)	2 tsp
black pepper	2.5 ml (½ tsp)	½ tsp
finely grated lemon rind	5 ml (1 tsp)	1 tsp

First make the stuffing: Melt butter in frying pan, add onion and cook until just tender. Add fennel, chives and ham. Cover and cook for 5 minutes. Remove from heat, add parsley, Pernod, pepper and lemon rind. Let mixture cool.

Prepare two large sheets of heavy-duty foil by rubbing them with oil. Place a fish on each and spoon fennel mixture into the cavity and over the fish. Bring edges of foil up and seal well.

Prepare an indirect fire and position the fish packets on the grid. Cover the kettle and cook for 20-25 minutes.

To serve: Unwrap fish and turn out onto a heated serving platter. Spoon juices over and serve immediately.

MARINATED SALMON (Serves 4)

Direct . . . 8 minutes

INGREDIENTS	METRIC/IMPERIAL	AMERICAN
salmon fillets	700 g (1½ lb)	1½ lb
sake	60 ml (4 tbsp)	4 tbsp
soy sauce	150 ml (5 fl oz)	⅔ cup
sweet white wine	100 ml (3½ fl oz)	½ cup
fresh ginger juice*	5 ml (1 tsp)	1 tsp

Remove skin and bones from the fish. Cut into about 24 cubes. Combine sake, soy sauce and wine. Marinate the salmon for 1 hour, then thread pieces onto four skewers. Reserve marinade.

Prepare a direct fire. Cook salmon for about 8 minutes, brushing with marinade and turning often so that the fish becomes well glazed. Remove from the coals and brush with ginger juice. Serve at once.

* See page 52

Blackened fish and Baked stuffed tomatoes (page 83)

sides with the seasoning mixture. Place the fillets on the hot pan (do not oil the pan) and drizzle a little extra butter onto the fish. Cook for 2-3 minutes until the fish is blackened, then turn and cook the other side, drizzling with a little more butter. Serve at once with the traditional Dirty Rice (page 78).

VARIATION
Blackened chicken breasts: Substitute chicken breasts for the fish fillets and cook them for 9 minutes, turning with tongs every 3 minutes. Serve with sour cream flavoured with salt, pepper and lemon juice.

* Available at speciality shops.

BLACKENED FISH (Serves 4)

Direct method . . . 6 minutes

Cajun-style food is very fashionable at the moment. This dish is ideal to cook outside.

INGREDIENTS	METRIC/IMPERIAL	AMERICAN
firm white fish fillets	1 kg (2¼ lb)	2¼ lb
butter, melted	75 g (2½ oz)	⅓ cup
SEASONING MIXTURE		
onion powder	7.5 ml (1½ tsp)	1½ tsp
garlic powder*	7.5 ml (1½ tsp)	1½ tsp
white pepper	7.5 ml (1½ tsp)	1½ tsp
cayenne pepper	7.5 ml (1½ tsp)	1½ tsp
dried thyme	7.5 ml (1½ tsp)	1½ tsp
dried oregano	5 ml (1 tsp)	1 tsp
salt	5 ml (1 tsp)	1 tsp

First make the seasoning mixture: Combine all the ingredients.
Prepare a direct fire, place a cast-iron frying pan or large flat grill on the grid over the coals. Cover the kettle and allow to heat for about 30 minutes. The pan must be extremely hot.
Brush the fillets with the melted butter and coat both

PORTUGUESE-STYLE PRAWNS
(Serves 6)

Direct . . . 8 minutes

INGREDIENTS	METRIC/IMPERIAL	AMERICAN
prawns (shrimps), cleaned but with heads intact	2 kg (4½ lb)	4½ lb
butter	300 g (11 oz)	1⅓ cups
Greek olive oil	150 ml (5 fl oz)	⅔ cup
tomato sauce	300 ml (11 fl oz)	1¼ cups
lemon juice	60 ml (4 tbsp)	4 tbsp
Worcestershire sauce	20 ml (4 tsp)	4 tsp
salt and black pepper		
garlic, crushed	3 cloves	3 cloves
Portuguese chilli (peri-peri) oil to taste (page 91)		
GARNISH		
lemon wedges		

Rinse the prawns and pat dry. Bring the remaining ingredients to the boil in a large saucepan. This may be done either on the stove or on the kettle. Add prawns and simmer for about 5 minutes, turning from time to time. The cooking time will depend on the size of the prawns. They are cooked when the shells turn deep pink and the flesh becomes opaque. Using a slotted spoon, drain the prawns well.
Prepare a direct fire and arrange the prawns on the grid directly over the coals. Barbecue for about 3 minutes, turning the prawns once during this time. Serve immediately with rice, lemon wedges and a salad. Reheat the remaining sauce and serve separately.

VEGETABLES & SALADS

Vegetables are often overlooked when barbecuing, but there are exciting ways to cook them on the barbecue kettle. Vegetables with thick skin, such as aubergines (eggplants or brinjals), peppers, onions, courgettes (zucchini or baby marrows), potatoes, pumpkins, butternut squashes and onions can be barbecued whole to retain their goodness, texture and flavour. A hinged grill is ideal for grilling small vegetables, while sliced vegetables can be threaded onto wooden skewers. A special rack to hold sweetcorn and potatoes fits around the edge of the grid, leaving the centre of the grid free for barbecuing other food. Vegetables can be baked in foil or ovenproof dish, and the cooking (Manchurian) grill cooks crunchy stir-fries that are great for a party.

Crisp salads are a natural accompaniment to barbecued foods. Serve light fruit and vegetable salads topped with crunchy nuts, sprouts and tangy dressings or hearty ones containing potatoes or rice; whatever your choice, ensure that the salads complement the main course by providing interesting contrasts in texture and flavour.

Left to right: Barbecue baked beans (page 82), Baked onions (page 82), Peppery bacon green salad (page 86) and Chopped Greek salad (page 85)

STUFFED GEM SQUASH (Serves 12)

Indirect . . . 50 minutes. Corn 'n' tater grill.

INGREDIENTS	METRIC/IMPERIAL	AMERICAN
gem squash	6	6
butter	45 ml (3 tbsp)	3 tbsp
Mozzarella cheese, grated	60 g (2 oz)	½ cup
spring (green) onions, including some of the green portion, chopped	1 bunch	1 bunch
salt and black pepper		

Prick the squash with a skewer, then fit into a corn 'n' tater grill.

Prepare an indirect fire and position the squash on the grid. Cover the kettle and cook for about 40 minutes, depending on the size and age of the squash. When cooked, cut in half and remove the seeds. Combine the remaining ingredients and spoon into the squash. Put the squash into a serving dish or foil drip pan. Return to the kettle and bake, covered, for 5-10 minutes, until heated through and the cheese has melted.

PAN-BAKED POTATO SLICES (Serves 4-6)

Indirect . . . 1 hour

There is no need to peel these potatoes if they have been well scrubbed.

INGREDIENTS	METRIC/IMPERIAL	AMERICAN
potatoes, thinly sliced	4-6	4-6
vegetable oil	60 ml (4 tbsp)	4 tbsp
salt and black pepper		

Rinse the sliced potatoes well. Dry with the help of a salad spinner. Turn into a bowl and add oil and seasonings, tossing to combine. Now turn into a foil drip pan. Place this pan between the coals under a suitable meat, for instance leg of lamb, shoulder of lamb or chicken. Cover the kettle and cook for about 1 hour, until the edges of the potatoes are crispy and brown.

VARIATION

Add 2.5 ml (½ tsp) herbs of your choice and 5 ml (1 tsp) dry mustard to the potatoes with the oil, salt and pepper. Bake as above, then pour 100 ml (3½ fl oz/½ cup) cream through the grid onto the potatoes during the last 20 minutes of the cooking time.

SMOKED BAKED POTATOES Brush whole potatoes with oil and place on the grid. Cover the kettle and cook for about 2 hours when smoking meat.

MANCHURIAN-STYLE STIR-FRY (Serves 8-10)

Direct . . . 10 minutes. Cooking (Manchurian) grill.

A really wonderful way to feed a crowd of teenagers. Provide a few egg slices (lifters) and let each person choose and cook their own favourite combination of ingredients.

INGREDIENTS	METRIC/IMPERIAL	AMERICAN
shredded cabbage	1 small	1 small
sliced onion	1 large	1 large
grated carrot	2-3	2-3
sliced leeks	2-3	2-3
grated courgettes (zucchini or baby marrows)	4-6	4-6
sliced mushrooms	10	10
sliced French (green) beans	250 g (9 oz)	2 cups
broccoli	150 g (5 oz)	1 cup
cauliflower	½ small	½ small
green peppers	1-2	1-2
sugarsnap peas	100 g (3½ oz)	½ cup
chicken, pork, beef or fish and shellfish	450 g (1 lb)	1 lb
vegetable oil		
garlic	2-3 cloves	2-3 cloves
soy sauce	75 ml (2½ fl oz)	⅓ cup
ginger ale or lemonade concentrate	45 ml (3 tbsp)	3 tbsp
Portuguese Chilli (peri-peri) Oil (page 91)	10-15 ml (2-3 tsp)	2-3 tsp
salt and black pepper		
OPTIONAL EXTRAS		
salted or spiced (peri-peri) cashew nuts	100 g (3½ oz)	1 cup
chopped chillies	2-3	2-3
sliced water chestnuts	200 g (7 oz)	½ cup
chopped bacon	6 rashers	6 slices

Prepare a direct fire. Place the cooking grill or wok over the coals and heat for a few minutes. Add a little oil, then the meat or fish of your choice. Fry for a few minutes. Slowly add a selection of vegetables and stir-fry for a few minutes before sprinkling with garlic, soy sauce, ginger ale or lemonade concentrate, Portuguese chilli (peri-peri) oil, salt and pepper. Now add a few optional extras and stir-fry for a few minutes more. Do not overcook the vegetables - they should still be crunchy.

Manchurian-style stir-fry

RATATOUILLE (Serves 6-8)

Indirect . . . 45 minutes.

INGREDIENTS	METRIC/IMPERIAL	AMERICAN
butter	75 g (2½ oz)	⅓ cup
onions, chopped	2	2
garlic, crushed	2 cloves	2 cloves
green peppers, chopped	2	2
aubergines (eggplants or brinjal), diced	2	2
courgettes (zucchini or baby marrows, thickly sliced	2-3	2-3
very ripe tomatoes, peeled and chopped	2-3	2-3
tomato purée	150 ml (5 fl oz)	⅔ cup
salt and black pepper		
sugar	5 ml (1 tsp)	1 tsp
chopped fresh basil	10 ml (2 tsp)	2 tsp
chopped fresh oregano	10 ml (2 tsp)	2 tsp
Italian olive oil	30 ml (2 tbsp)	2 tbsp
chopped fresh parsley	30 ml (2 tbsp)	2 tbsp
grated Parmesan cheese	30 ml (2 tbsp)	2 tbsp

Prepare an indirect fire and place the grid in position. Place a heavy cast-iron casserole directly over the coals and heat the butter. Add onion, garlic and green pepper and sauté for about 5 minutes. Add aubergines and courgettes and sauté for a few minutes more. Stir in tomatoes, tomato purée, salt, pepper, sugar and herbs. Cover the casserole and place it in the centre of the grid. Cover the kettle and bake for 30-40 minutes until the vegetables are soft. Stir in the oil and parsley, and sprinkle with cheese. Serve either as a vegetarian meal or as a meat accompaniment.

ROAST PUMPKIN (Serves 6-8)

Indirect . . . 45 minutes

INGREDIENTS	METRIC/IMPERIAL	AMERICAN
pumpkin, peeled	8 slices	8 slices
vegetable oil		
salt and black pepper		

Place pumpkin in a foil drip pan, brush with oil, then sprinkle with salt and pepper. Place the pumpkin in the kettle under the accompanying meat or chicken. Cover the kettle and cook for about 45 minutes, until well browned. Alternatively, place the brushed and seasoned pumpkin on a piece of foil. Turn up the edges of the foil to prevent the juice from running out. Cook on the grid next to the meat for 45-60 minutes.

DIRTY RICE (Serves 8)

Direct; Indirect . . . 40 minutes

INGREDIENTS	METRIC/IMPERIAL	AMERICAN
vegetable oil	30 ml (2 tbsp)	2 tbsp
chicken livers, finely chopped	150 g (5 oz)	1 cup
pork, minced (ground)	150 g (5 oz)	1¼ cups
onion, chopped	1	1
green pepper, chopped	1 small	1 small
celery, chopped	2 sticks	2 stalks
garlic, crushed	1 clove	1 clove
salt	2.5 ml (½ tsp)	½ tsp
cayenne pepper	1-2.5 ml (¼-½ tsp)	¼-½ tsp
black pepper		
chicken stock	190 ml (6½ fl oz)	¾ cup
boiling water	375 ml (13 fl oz)	1½ cup
rice	175 g (6 oz)	¾ cup

Prepare a direct fire. Heat the oil in a small saucepan over the coals, add chicken livers, pork, onion, green pepper, celery, garlic and seasonings. Sauté for about 10 minutes, then add the chicken stock and cook for 5 minutes. Remove and set aside.

Combine water and rice in a cast-iron casserole and cover with a lid. Re-arrange the coals to form an indirect fire and replace the grid. Put the casserole in the centre of the grid, cover the kettle and cook for 15 minutes. Now stir in the meat mixture. Cover the casserole and the kettle and allow to cook for a further 10-15 minutes until the rice is tender.

HINT: If you want the rice to stand for some time before serving, be sure not to overcook it. When just cooked, remove from the heat but do not lift the lid. The rice will stay piping hot for at least 30 minutes.

BUTTERED COURGETTES (Serves 4)

Direct . . . 10 minutes.

INGREDIENTS	METRIC/IMPERIAL	AMERICAN
courgettes (zucchini or baby marrows)	8 small	8 small
SAUCE		
butter or margarine	125 g (4 oz)	½ cup
hot mustard	10 ml (2 tsp)	2 tsp
freshly grated root ginger	5 ml (1 tsp)	1 tsp
garlic, crushed	1 small clove	1 small clove
lemon juice	5 ml (1 tsp)	1 tsp

Slice the courgettes diagonally into large chunks. To make the sauce: Melt the butter and stir in the remaining sauce ingredients.

Prepare a direct fire or use an existing hot fire. Place

courgettes on a sheet of heavy-duty foil (and turn up the edges) or in a foil drip pan. Place the foil or drip pan over the hot coals and brush the vegetables with the butter sauce. Cover the foil container and the kettle and cook for about 10 minutes, or until the vegetables are just tender, brushing frequently with the butter sauce.

FARM-STYLE SWEETCORN (Serves 8)

Indirect . . . 1 hour

INGREDIENTS	METRIC/IMPERIAL	AMERICAN
sweetcorn, with husks	8	8
butter	100 g (3½ oz)	⅓ cup
salt and black pepper		
Marmite (yeast extract)	15-20 ml (3-4 tsp)	3-4 tsp

Soak the sweetcorn in a large basin of water for 15 minutes.

Prepare an indirect fire and fit a foil drip pan between the coals. Put the grid in position and then lay the drained sweetcorn down the centre of the grid. Cover the kettle and cook for 45-60 minutes, depending on the size of the cobs. Combine butter, seasonings and Marmite. Remove husks from sweetcorn and serve with butter mixture.

BLACK MUSHROOMS DELUXE
(Serves 8)

Direct; Indirect . . . 22 minutes

INGREDIENTS	METRIC/IMPERIAL	AMERICAN
black mushrooms	8 large	8 large
butter	100 g (3½ oz)	⅓ cup
garlic, crushed	2 cloves	2 cloves
chopped fresh parsley	30 ml (2 tbsp)	2 tbsp
chopped fresh thyme	2.5 ml (½ tsp)	½ tsp
sweet sherry	30 ml (2 tbsp)	2 tbsp
salt and black pepper		

Wipe the mushrooms, cut off the stems, chop them and set aside. Arrange the mushrooms either in a foil drip pan or in a casserole. Melt the butter and add the remaining ingredients, including the chopped stems. Spoon onto the mushrooms and cover.

Prepare an indirect fire and place the covered drip pan or casserole on the grid directly over the coals. Cover the kettle and bake for about 7 minutes, then move the drip pan or casserole to the centre of the grid and bake, covered, for 10-15 minutes more, depending on the size of the mushrooms.

POLENTA (Serves 6)

Direct   30-50 minutes.

This corn staple is eaten in many countries and has a variety of names, but whatever it's called it goes well with barbecued meat.

INGREDIENTS	METRIC/IMPERIAL	AMERICAN
water	500 ml (18 fl oz)	2 cups
salt	5 ml (1 tsp)	1 tsp
corn meal (maize meal)	175 g (6 oz)	¾ cup
butter or margarine	60 g (2 oz)	¼ cup

Bring the water and salt to the boil in an ovenproof casserole, then add corn meal. Cover and boil for 5 minutes. Stir thoroughly, then replace the lid. Place the casserole over medium coals, cover the kettle and steam for at least 25 minutes, or longer if desired. When ready to serve, stir in butter.

VARIATION

Follow the recipe above, and steam on the barbecue kettle for 25 minutes. Stir in 250 g (9 oz/1 cup) frozen sweetcorn and 100 g (3½ oz/½ cup) butter. Mix well and steam for another 20 minutes, stirring in a little more butter if desired.

SWEETCORN PARCELS (Serves 8)

Direct . . . 15 minutes.

These make an excellent start to a meal too.

INGREDIENTS	METRIC/IMPERIAL	AMERICAN
sweetcorn	8	8
red peppers	2 small	2 small
butter	200 g (7 oz)	¾ cup
paprika	2.5 ml (½ tsp)	½ tsp
cayenne pepper	pinch	pinch
salt and black pepper		
chopped fresh parsley	60 ml (4 tbsp)	4 tbsp

Cut 8 large pieces of foil and fold each in half. Place an ear of sweetcorn on each piece. Seed and chop the red peppers very finely. Combine with butter, paprika, cayenne, salt, black pepper and parsley. Spread butter mixture generously on sweetcorn, roll foil up tightly and seal the parcels (packages).

Prepare a direct fire and arrange the parcels on the grid directly over the coals. Cover the kettle and bake for 15 minutes. Serve piping hot.

SMOKED SWEETCORN Remove husks and silk from sweetcorn. Place on the grid or in a corn 'n' tater grill in a covered kettle for about 20 minutes while smoking meat.

GIANT PIZZA (Serves 8)

Direct . . . 10 minutes. Cooking (Manchurian) grill.

INGREDIENTS	METRIC/IMPERIAL	AMERICAN
plain (cake) flour	500 g (18 oz)	4 cups
salt	5 ml (1 tsp)	1 tsp
instant yeast	15 g (½ oz)	1 tbsp
sugar	5 ml (1 tsp)	1 tsp
vegetable oil	100 ml (3½ fl oz)	½ cup
warm water	240 ml (8½ fl oz)	1 cup
TOMATO BASE		
vegetable oil	75 ml (2½ fl oz)	⅓ cup
onion, chopped	1	1
garlic, crushed	2 cloves	2 cloves
canned peeled tomatoes	750 g (1½ lb)	1½ lb
salt and black pepper		
dried oregano	10 ml (2 tsp)	2 tsp
sugar	10 ml (2 tsp)	2 tsp
bay leaves	2	2
TOPPING		
salami		
olives		
capers		
anchovies		
mushrooms		
green pepper		
seafood		
Mozzarella cheese, sliced	650 g-1 kg (1½-2¼ lb)	1½-2¼ lb

Sift flour and salt and then add yeast, sugar, oil and water. Using the dough hook, mix for about 4 minutes to a firm, smooth dough. Place the dough in an oiled plastic bag and leave in a warm place until doubled in bulk.

Roll out the dough as large as possible. Place on a well-oiled cooking grill, pressing the dough out to fit. Form a slightly raised edge to keep the filling in place. Spread the dough with the tomato base mixture, then sprinkle with topping ingredients of your choice. Top generously with Mozzarella cheese. Stand in a warm place for 15 minutes.

To make the tomato base: Heat the oil in a saucepan, add onion and garlic and sauté for a few minutes. Add remaining ingredients and bring to the boil. Simmer with the lid off for 15-20 minutes until the mixture has thickened. Allow to cool before using.

Prepare a direct fire and allow the coals to go almost out. Spreading the coals around will help decrease the heat. The fire must be very low, otherwise the dough will burn before the topping has cooked. Place the cooking grill on the fire, cover the kettle and cook for about 10 minutes, then slice and serve.

HINT

To slice Mozzarella cheese thinly, place in the deep freeze until hard but not frozen. Using a food processor fitted with a slicing plate, slice the cheese. The cheese may then be used or frozen until required. Boneless chicken breasts, beef, pork, fish and so on may also be sliced using this technique.

MIXED VEGETABLE POT (Serves 6-8)

Indirect . . . 1 hour 10 minutes

The vegetables suggested in this recipe are only a general guide; use any fresh vegetables of your choice.

INGREDIENTS	METRIC/IMPERIAL	AMERICAN
new potatoes, well scrubbed	12	12
onions	12 small	12 small
butternut squash, peeled and diced	1 medium	1 medium
carrots, thickly sliced	2	2
parsnips or turnips, diced	2	2
aubergine (eggplant or brinjal), cubed	1 large	1 large
French (green) beans, cut into 4-cm (1½-in) pieces	250 g (9 oz)	1½ cups
unpeeled garlic	6 cloves	6 cloves
butter, melted	45 ml (3 tbsp)	3 tbsp
olive oil, preferably Italian	30 ml (2 tbsp)	2 tbsp
salt and black pepper		
water	45 ml (3 tbsp)	3 tbsp
fresh herbs (thyme, oregano, or basil)	large sprigs	large sprigs
courgettes (zucchini or baby marrows), thickly sliced	3	3
mushrooms, halved	200 g (7 oz)	2¾ cup

Lightly oil a large cast-iron casserole. Layer the vegetables, beginning with the potatoes, then onions, butternut squash, carrots, parsnips, aubergine and beans. Add the *unpeeled* garlic cloves, then combine butter and oil and pour over the vegetables. Sprinkle lightly with salt and pepper, add the water and top with herbs. Cover with a well-fitting lid.

Prepare an indirect fire and fit the grid. Place the casserole in the centre of the grid. Cover the kettle and bake for about 1 hour - until the vegetables are tender. Now add courgettes and mushrooms, cover the casserole and the kettle and cook for a further 10-15 minutes. Remove garlic. Serve as a vegetarian meal or as an accompaniment to roast meat.

Giant pizza

Baked Onions (Serves 6)

Direct . . . 20 minutes.

INGREDIENTS	METRIC/IMPERIAL	AMERICAN
onions, unpeeled	6	6
vegetable oil	30 ml (2 tbsp)	2 tbsp
salt and black pepper		
dried thyme	2.5 ml (½ tsp)	½ tsp
butter	45 ml (3 tbsp)	3 tbsp

Cut the onions in half lengthways and brush all over with oil. Place onions either on a large piece of heavy-duty foil or in a foil drip pan. Season lightly with salt and pepper, sprinkle with thyme and dot with butter. Cover the pan or fold the foil into a parcel.

Prepare a direct fire and place the onions on the grid directly over the coals. Cover the kettle and cook for 20 minutes until onions are tender and golden brown.

Chow Faan Rice (Serves 6)

INGREDIENTS	METRIC/IMPERIAL	AMERICAN
streaky bacon, chopped	5 rashers	5 slices
cold cooked rice	500 g (18 oz)	4 cups
soy sauce	30 ml (2 tbsp)	2 tbsp
snipped chives	45 ml (3 tbsp)	3 tbsp
eggs	2	2
milk	30 ml (2 tbsp)	2 tbsp

Fry the bacon until crispy, then drain and set aside. Add rice to the bacon fat, adding a little oil if necessary, and fry for a couple of minutes. Stir in soy sauce, chives and bacon, and cook to heat through. Lightly beat eggs and milk, stir into the rice and cook for a few minutes more, stirring all the time.

NOTE: Use a cast-iron casserole or, if there are a large number of people, a cooking (Manchurian) grill to cook this dish directly over the coals, just before serving.

Butternut Squash With Cumin (Serves 4-6)

Indirect . . . 1 hour

INGREDIENTS	METRIC/IMPERIAL	AMERICAN
butternut squash	2	2
butter	100 g (3½ oz)	⅓ cup
cumin seeds, crushed	5 ml (1 tsp)	1 tsp
salt and black pepper		
paprika		

Prepare an indirect fire and fit a foil drip pan between the coals. Prick the squashes well, and then place on the grid over the drip pan. Cover the kettle and cook for 30-45 minutes, depending on the size of the vegetables. When cooked, remove from the kettle, cut in half and scoop out the seeds. Add plenty of butter to each half. Sprinkle with cumin, seasonings and paprika. Return to the kettle and bake, covered, for a further 10 minutes.

NOTE: If the centre of the kettle is being used, place butternuts on the corn 'n' tater holder to cook.

Baked Sweet Potatoes (Serves 8)

Indirect . . . 1 hour. Corn 'n' tater grill.

INGREDIENTS	METRIC/IMPERIAL	AMERICAN
sweet potatoes	8 medium	8 medium
little vegetable oil		
butter	60 ml (4 tbsp)	4 tbsp
salt and black pepper		
brown sugar	45 ml (3 tbsp)	3 tbsp

Wash the potatoes well and brush very lightly with oil. Place potatoes in the corn 'n' tater grill.

Prepare an indirect fire. Place the potatoes in the centre of the grid, cover the kettle and cook for about 1 hour, until tender. Remove potatoes from the kettle, cut off the tops and break up the cooked flesh slightly with a fork. Add a little butter, salt and pepper and brown sugar to each potato. Serve piping hot.

Barbecue Baked Beans (Serves 8)

Direct . . . 30 minutes.

INGREDIENTS	METRIC/IMPERIAL	AMERICAN
canned baked beans in tomato sauce	750 g (1½ lb)	1½ lb
ginger biscuit (cookie) crumbs	60 ml (4 tbsp)	4 tbsp
tomato sauce	90 ml (3 oz)	⅓ cup
black treacle (molasses)	45 ml (3 tbsp)	3 tbsp
brown sugar	30 ml (2 tbsp)	2 tbsp
finely chopped onion	30 ml (2 tbsp)	2 tbsp
black pepper		
bacon	4 rashers	4 slices

Combine beans, crumbs, tomato sauce, black treacle, sugar, onion and pepper. Turn into a heavy cast-iron saucepan and place over the hot coals. Cut bacon into 2-cm (¾-in) pieces and stir into the beans. Cover saucepan and kettle and cook for about 30 minutes, or until bubbling.

SWEETCORN FRITTERS   (Serves 6-8)

Direct . . . 10 minutes. Cooking (Manchurian) grill.

These make an excellent addition to a breakfast party. They are also good as part of a barbecue.

INGREDIENTS	METRIC/IMPERIAL	AMERICAN
cake (plain) flour	125 g (4 oz)	1 cup
baking powder	15 ml (1 tbsp)	1 tbsp
salt	2.5 ml (½ tsp)	½ tsp
dry mustard	2.5 ml (½ tsp)	½ tsp
eggs, lightly beaten	2	2
milk	375 ml (13 fl oz)	1½ cups
butter, melted	30 ml (2 tbsp)	2 tbsp
ham, chopped	125 g (4 oz)	4 oz
drained whole kernel sweetcorn	175 g (6 oz)	1 cup
vegetable oil		

Sift the dry ingredients. Combine eggs and milk, add to dry ingredients and beat until smooth. Stir in the butter, ham and sweetcorn.

Prepare a direct fire, fit a cooking grill and allow to become hot. Brush with oil, then drop spoonfuls of the mixture onto the grill. When bubbles appear on the surface, turn the fritters over and brown the other side. Serve immediately.

PILAU RICE   (Serves 6)

Indirect . . . 30 minutes

INGREDIENTS	METRIC/IMPERIAL	AMERICAN
butter or ghee	90 g (3 oz)	⅓ cup
onion, chopped	1	1
whole cardamoms	4	4
stick cinnamon	small piece	small piece
whole cloves	3	3
turmeric	2.5 ml (½ tsp)	½ tsp
bay leaf	1	1
salt	5 ml (1 tsp)	1 tsp
long grain rice	275 g (11 oz)	1½ cups
water	750 ml (1¼ pints)	3 cups

Heat the butter or ghee in a casserole dish and fry the onion until golden brown. Add all the spices, bay leaf and salt and fry carefully for 2 minutes. Stir in the rice and fry for a few minutes more. Add water, cover and bring to the boil. Simmer for about 20 minutes, until rice is tender. Remove lid and cook in the kettle with Tandoori Chicken (page 58) for 10 minutes.

NOTE: This dish may be prepared in advance up to adding the water. It may then be cooked in a covered casserole in the kettle with the chicken for 25-30 minutes. When rice is tender, remove lid and allow rice to dry out.

BAKED STUFFED TOMATOES
(SERVES 8)

Indirect . . . 15 minutes

INGREDIENTS	METRIC/IMPERIAL	AMERICAN
tomatoes	8	8
fresh brown breadcrumbs	60 g (2 oz)	1 cup
butter	45 ml (3 tbsp)	3 tbsp
onion, chopped	1 small	1 small
bacon, chopped	2 rashers	2 slices
salt and black pepper		
sugar	5 ml (1 tsp)	1 tsp
chopped fresh parsley	30 ml (2 tbsp)	2 tbsp
grated Cheddar cheese	75 g (2½ oz)	¾ cup

Cut tops off tomatoes and scoop out the pulp into a bowl. Add breadcrumbs. Heat butter and sauté onion and bacon. Now combine all the ingredients and pile into the tomato shells and arrange in a foil drip pan.

Prepare an indirect fire and position the drip pan in the centre of the grid. Cover the kettle and cook for 10-15 minutes, depending on the size of the tomatoes.

BAKED PUMPKIN   (Serves 8-10)

Indirect . . . 1½ hours

INGREDIENTS	METRIC/IMPERIAL	AMERICAN
whole pumpkin	1	1
butter	100 g (3½ oz)	⅓ cup
salt and black pepper		
Gruyère cheese, grated	200 g (7 oz)	1½ cups

Prepare an indirect fire and fit a foil drip pan between the coals.

Prick the pumpkin all over and place it on the grid over the drip pan. Cover the kettle and bake for 1-1½ hours, depending on the size of the pumpkin. When cooked, cut off the top and scoop out the seeds. Loosen flesh and mash in the shell with butter and seasonings. Mix in the cheese. Replace the pumpkin lid and return to the kettle. Bake, covered, for a further 10 minutes before serving.

Left to right: Eastern potato salad, Cucumber, walnut and dill salad (page 87) and Tangy cabbage salad

SALADS

EASTERN POTATO SALAD (Serves 6)

INGREDIENTS	METRIC/IMPERIAL	AMERICAN
small new potatoes	750 g (1½ lb)	1½ lb
vegetable oil	30 ml (2 tbsp)	2 tbsp
mustard seeds	5 ml (1 tsp)	1 tsp
caraway seeds	1 ml (¼ tsp)	¼ tsp
onion, finely chopped	1 small	1 small
garlic, finely chopped	1 clove	1 clove
chopped fresh coriander (cilantro)	15 ml (1 tbsp)	1 tbsp
grated fresh root ginger	5 ml (1 tsp)	1 tsp
chopped green chilli pepper	2.5 ml (½ tsp)	½ tsp
turmeric	2.5 ml (½ tsp)	½ tsp
ground cumin	1 ml (¼ tsp)	¼ tsp
salt	2.5 ml (½ tsp)	½ tsp
natural yoghurt	250 ml (9 fl oz)	1 cup
chopped fresh coriander (cilantro) to garnish		

Cook the potatoes in boiling salted water until tender. Cool, peel and cut into small cubes. Heat the oil, add mustard and caraway seeds and stir for about 1 minute. Reduce heat, add onion, garlic, coriander, ginger, chilli pepper, turmeric, cumin and potatoes. Mix gently to coat potatoes. Season with salt. Place mixture in a bowl, stir in yoghurt and chill, covered, for several hours or overnight. Serve garnished with coriander.

SUGARSNAP PEAS WITH CORIANDER (Serves 6-8)

INGREDIENTS	METRIC/IMPERIAL	AMERICAN
sugarsnap peas	500 g (18 oz)	3 cups
red wine vinegar	50 ml (3 tbsp)	3 tbsp
Dijon mustard	10 ml (2 tsp)	2 tsp
chilli pepper, seeded and crushed	1	1
grated fresh root ginger	5 ml (1 tsp)	1 tsp
salt and pepper		
vegetable oil	60 ml (4 tbsp)	4 tbsp
onion, sliced	1 small	1 small
red pepper, diced	1 small	1 small
fresh coriander (cilantro) leaves	90 g (3 oz)	1 cup
lettuce	1 small head	1 small head

sized cubes. Place potatoes in a large bowl and toss with the vinegar. Add beans, spring onions, salt and pepper to taste. In a food processor, combine mustard, mayonnaise, oil and roasted pepper. Process until mixture is smooth. Spoon over vegetables and toss gently to coat.

TANGY CABBAGE SALAD (Serves 10-12)

INGREDIENTS	METRIC/IMPERIAL	AMERICAN
cabbage	1 kg (2¼ lb)	2¼ lb
turnip	1 small	1 small
carrots	2	2
radishes	1 small bunch	1 small bunch
onion, chopped	½	½
chopped fresh parsley	60 ml (4 tbsp)	4 tbsp
chopped fresh tarragon	5 ml (1 tsp)	1 tsp
or dried	2.5 ml (½ tsp)	½ tsp
chopped fresh thyme	2.5 ml (½ tsp)	½ tsp
or dried	1 ml (¼ tsp)	¼ tsp
mayonnaise	250 ml (9 fl oz)	1 cup
cider vinegar	100 ml (3½ fl oz)	½ cup
lemon juice	15 ml (1 tbsp)	1 tbsp
sugar	5 ml (1 tsp)	1 tsp
black pepper	1 ml (¼ tsp)	¼ tsp
white pepper	pinch	pinch
Tabasco sauce	few drops	few drops
salt	2.5 ml (½ tsp)	½ tsp

Shred the cabbage, turnip, carrots and radishes into a large bowl. Add onion, parsley, tarragon and thyme and toss to mix. Combine mayonnaise, vinegar, lemon juice, sugar, black and white peppers, Tabasco sauce and salt. Mix well, then pour over vegetables. Mix thoroughly, then chill for at least 36 hours. Stir well just before serving.

Blanch peas in salted boiling water for 1 minute. Drain and refresh under running cold water. Drain and chill. Combine vinegar, mustard, chilli pepper, ginger, salt and pepper. Beat in the oil. Add onion and red pepper to the peas. Add dressing and toss well. Just before serving, gently stir in the coriander leaves and serve in a lettuce-lined bowl.

POTATO AND BEAN SALAD (Serves 6-8)

INGREDIENTS	METRIC/IMPERIAL	AMERICAN
red pepper	1 large	1 large
potatoes	750 g (1½ lb)	1½ lb
red wine vinegar	30 ml (2 tbsp)	2 tbsp
canned butter beans, drained	400 g (14 oz)	2 cups
chopped spring (green) onions	30 ml (2 tbsp)	2 tbsp
salt and pepper		
Dijon mustard	5 ml (1 tsp)	1 tsp
mayonnaise	125 ml (4 fl oz)	½ cup
vegetable oil	30 ml (2 tbsp)	2 tbsp

Roast the pepper over hot coals or under the grill until charred all over, turning frequently. Cover with foil and stand for 10 minutes, then peel the pepper and remove core and seeds. Cook unpeeled potatoes in boiling salted water until tender. Drain and cut into bite-

CHOPPED GREEK SALAD (Serves 6)

INGREDIENTS	METRIC/IMPERIAL	AMERICAN
lettuce, shredded	1 small head	1 small head
cucumber, diced	½	½
green pepper, diced	1 small	1 small
spring (green) onions, chopped	1 bunch	1 bunch
tomatoes, diced	2	2
feta cheese, diced	60 g (2 oz)	2 oz
Herb Salad Dressing (page 88)		

Combine all the ingredients, toss gently and serve with Greek-style Leg of Lamb (page 26) and Pitta Breads (page 104).

ITALIAN RICE SALAD (Serves 6-8)

INGREDIENTS	METRIC/IMPERIAL	AMERICAN
long-grain rice	400 g (14 oz)	2 cups
water	1 litre (1¾ pints)	4 cups
butter or margarine	30 ml (2 tbsp)	2 tbsp
chicken stock cube	1½	1½
or chicken stock powder	15 ml (1 tbsp)	1 tbsp
turmeric	2.5 ml (½ tsp)	½ tsp
salt and pepper		
Italian salad dressing	90 ml (3 fl oz)	⅓ cup
vegetable oil	30 ml (2 tbsp)	2 tbsp
onion, diced	1	1
red peppers, diced	2	2
green peppers, diced	3	3
mushrooms, sliced	200 g (7 oz)	2¾ cups
stuffed green olives, sliced	75 g (2½ oz)	½ cup
lemon juice	30 ml (2 tbsp)	2 tbsp

Place rice, water, butter or margarine, chicken stock cube or powder, turmeric and 5 ml (1 tsp) salt in a large saucepan. Bring to the boil, then reduce heat, cover and simmer for about 20 minutes, or until rice is tender and liquid has been absorbed. Place rice in a large bowl and add salad dressing.

Heat oil in a frying pan and cook onion until tender. Stir in red and green peppers and season with salt and pepper. Cook, stirring, until peppers are just tender, then add mushrooms and cook for 1 minute. Drain well and add to the rice with the olives and lemon juice. Mix gently, then chill well for about 2 hours before serving.

PEPPERY BACON GREEN SALAD
(Serves 8)

INGREDIENTS	METRIC/IMPERIAL	AMERICAN
butterhead (cabbage) lettuce	2 heads	2 heads
fresh spinach	200 g (7 oz)	3 cups
mushrooms, sliced	200 g (7 oz)	2¾ cups
bean sprouts	60 g (2 oz)	1 cup
bacon, fried and diced	8 rashers	8 slices
blue cheese, crumbled	125 g (4 oz)	¾ cup
hard-boiled eggs, sliced	2	2
cherry (baby) tomatoes, halved		
fresh basil leaves, chopped	6	6

DRESSING

	METRIC/IMPERIAL	AMERICAN
sour cream	190 ml (6½ fl oz)	¾ cup
mayonnaise	60 ml (4 tbsp)	4 tbsp
lemon juice	30 ml (2 tbsp)	2 tbsp
Worcestershire sauce	5 ml (1 tsp)	1 tsp
beef stock cube	1	1
or beef stock powder	5 ml (1 tsp)	1 tsp
warm water	20 ml (4 tsp)	4 tsp
salt		
coarsely ground peppercorns	15 ml (1 tbsp)	1 tbsp

First make the dressing: Combine all ingredients, except the milk, mixing well. If too thick, thin down with a little milk. Chill for at least 2 hours.

To make the salad: Tear lettuce and spinach into bite-sized pieces and place in a large bowl. Add mushrooms. Add dressing and toss to mix. Top with bean sprouts, bacon, cheese and egg slices. Garnish with tomato halves and sprinkle with basil. Serve at once.

PINEAPPLE SALAD (Serves 8-10)

This unusual salad goes well with poultry or pork.

INGREDIENTS	METRIC/IMPERIAL	AMERICAN
pineapple, peeled and cored	1	1
marshmallows, quartered	175 g (6 oz)	2 cups
slivered almonds, toasted	100 g (3½ oz)	1 cup
seedless grapes	150 g (5 oz)	1 cup
banana, sliced	1	1
lemon juice		
sour cream	250 ml (9 fl oz)	1 cup
mayonnaise	125 ml (4 fl oz)	½ cup
canned stoned (pitted) black cherries, drained	400 g (14 oz)	2½ cups

DRESSING

	METRIC/IMPERIAL	AMERICAN
pineapple juice	250 ml (9 fl oz)	1 cup
sugar	75 g (2½ oz)	⅓ cup
lemon juice	75 ml (2½ fl oz)	⅓ cup
egg yolks, lightly beaten	3 large	3 large
grated lemon rind	15 ml (1 tbsp)	1 tbsp

Cut pineapple into bite-sized pieces and combine with marshmallows, almonds and grapes in a large bowl. Sprinkle banana with a little lemon juice and add to the bowl. Stir in the sour cream and mayonnaise. Chill for several hours or overnight.

To make the dressing: Combine all ingredients, except lemon rind, in a double boiler. Cook gently, stirring, until thick. Remove from heat, stir in lemon rind and cool before serving.

To serve: Stir cherries into pineapple salad and turn into a decorative bowl. Serve dressing separately.

Feta And Vegetable Salad
(Serves 6)

INGREDIENTS	METRIC/IMPERIAL	AMERICAN
cauliflower, broken into florets (flowerets)	1 head	1 head
pattypan squash	6	6
courgettes (zucchini or baby marrows)	4	4
salt		
red pepper, cut in julienne strips	1	1
vegetable oil	75 ml (2½ fl oz)	⅓ cup
tarragon vinegar	60 ml (4 tbsp)	4 tbsp
chopped fresh parsley	30 ml (2 tbsp)	2 tbsp
chopped fresh dill	10 ml (2 tsp)	2 tsp
or dried	2.5 ml (½ tsp)	½ tsp
sugar	5 ml (1 tsp)	1 tsp
pepper		
feta cheese, cubed	250 g (9 oz)	1¾ cups
ripe olives	150 g (5 oz)	1 cup

If cauliflower florets are large, cut into bite-sized pieces. Quarter pattypan squash and slice courgettes thickly. Bring a large saucepan of salted water to the boil. Add cauliflower, cook for 3 minutes and remove. Cook pattypans for 3 minutes and remove. Add courgettes, cook 2 minutes and remove. Refresh cauliflower, pattypans and courgettes in cold water, then drain well. Add red pepper to the saucepan and cook 1 minute, remove and refresh in cold water. Drain. Place vegetables in a large bowl.

Combine oil, vinegar, herbs, sugar and pepper to taste and mix well. Add feta and olives to the vegetables. Add the dressing and toss gently to coat. Cover and chill for at least 1 hour.

Cucumber, Walnut And Dill Salad   (Serves 8-10)

INGREDIENTS	METRIC/IMPERIAL	AMERICAN
walnuts, toasted*	100 g (3½ oz)	1 cup
natural yoghurt	1 litre (1¾ pints)	4 cups
sour cream	250 ml (9 fl oz)	1 cup
lemon juice	10 ml (2 tsp)	2 tsp
cucumbers (English)	3	3
chopped fresh dill	60 ml (4 tbsp)	4 tbsp
or dried	20 ml (4 tsp)	4 tsp
salt and black pepper		
cayenne pepper	pinch	pinch
finely grated lemon rind	2.5 ml (½ tsp)	½ tsp

Chop nuts coarsely and set aside. Combine yoghurt, sour cream and lemon juice, and set aside. Peel, seed and finely dice the cucumbers and add to the yoghurt with the dill, salt and pepper to taste, cayenne pepper and lemon rind. Chill mixture for at least 2 hours. Just before serving stir in the walnuts. Delicious served with spicy kebabs and other meat dishes.

* Place walnuts on a baking sheet in the oven at 160 °C (325 °F/gas 2) for 5 minutes. Cool before using.

Sweetcorn Salad   (Serves 6-8)

INGREDIENTS	METRIC/IMPERIAL	AMERICAN
frozen sweetcorn kernels	350 g (12 oz)	3 cups
red pepper, cut in julienne strips	1	1
green pepper, cut in julienne strips	1	1
courgettes (zucchini or baby marrows), cut in julienne strips	2	2
aubergine (eggplant or brinjal), cut in julienne strips	1 small	1 small
spring (green) onions, halved lengthways	1 bunch	1 bunch
butterhead (cabbage) lettuce	1 head	1 head
red lettuce (lollo rosso)	1 head	1 head
chopped fresh parsley	15 ml (1 tbsp)	1 tbsp
chopped fresh thyme	5 ml (1 tsp)	1 tsp
tarragon vinegar	125 ml (4 fl oz)	½ cup
vegetable oil, or walnut oil	125 ml (4 fl oz)	½ cup
salt and pepper		

Blanch sweetcorn in boiling water for 2 minutes, then drain and refresh in cold water. Blanch red pepper for 1 minute, and refresh. Repeat with green pepper. Blanch courgettes, then aubergines and refresh, keeping each vegetable separate.

Tear lettuce leaves into bite-sized pieces, toss with parsley and thyme and arrange on a large platter.

Combine vinegar, oil, salt and pepper to taste and pour over sweetcorn. Toss to mix, then drain, reserving the dressing. Arrange sweetcorn in rays to resemble spokes of a wheel on the lettuce. Add each vegetable separately to the dressing, toss and drain. Arrange vegetables between 'spokes' of sweetcorn. Pour any remaining dressing over the salad.

SALAD DRESSINGS, SAUCES & SAVOURY BUTTERS

ROASTED PEPPER MAYONNAISE
(Makes about 375 ml/13 fl oz/1½ cups)

Direct . . . 30 minutes

Delicious with poultry or beef.

INGREDIENTS	METRIC/IMPERIAL	AMERICAN
red peppers	2	2
egg yolks	2	2
wine vinegar	15 ml (1 tbsp)	1 tbsp
juice of ½ a lemon		
soy sauce	2.5 ml (½ tsp)	½ tsp
white pepper	pinch	pinch
Dijon mustard	7.5 ml (1½ tsp)	1½ tsp
vegetable oil	250 ml (9 fl oz)	1 cup
Tabasco sauce	few drops	few drops
spring (green) onions, finely chopped	2	2
boiling water	15 ml (1 tbsp)	1 tbsp

Cook peppers in boiling water for about 2 minutes, then drain.

Prepare a direct fire and place peppers on grid. Cover the kettle and roast the peppers, turning frequently, until they are charred and soft, about 25-30 minutes. Peel peppers, remove stem, seeds and ribs. Dice finely.

Place egg yolks in a blender or food processor and add vinegar, lemon juice, soy sauce, pepper and mustard. Blend for a few seconds, then with the motor still running, slowly add the oil in a steady stream. Add Tabasco sauce, spring onion, boiling water and peppers and blend to mix. Refrigerate until required.

In a food processor, combine egg yolks, vinegar, lemon juice, salt, pepper, garlic, nutmeg and parsley. Blend until well mixed. With the motor running, slowly add the oil and blend until thickened. Mix in mustard and chives. Adjust seasoning if necessary.

MUSTARD DRESSING
(Makes about 500 ml/18 fl oz/2¼ cups)

Delicious on salads.

INGREDIENTS	METRIC/IMPERIAL	AMERICAN
egg yolks	3	3
red wine vinegar	30 ml (2 tbsp)	2 tbsp
lemon juice	15 ml (1 tbsp)	1 tbsp
salt	2.5 ml (½ tsp)	½ tsp
black pepper	2.5 ml (½ tsp)	½ tsp
garlic	½ small clove	½ small clove
grated nutmeg	pinch	pinch
chopped fresh parsley	10 ml (2 tsp)	2 tsp
vegetable oil	375 ml (13 fl oz)	1½ cups
Dijon mustard	40 ml (8 tsp)	8 tsp
chopped chives	15 ml (1 tbsp)	1 tbsp

HERB SALAD DRESSING
(Makes about 125 ml/4 fl oz/½ cup)

INGREDIENTS	METRIC/IMPERIAL	AMERICAN
vegetable oil	75 ml (2½ fl oz)	⅓ cup
white wine vinegar	40 ml (8 tsp)	8 tsp
salt and black pepper		
chopped fresh thyme	2.5 ml (½ tsp)	½ tsp
chopped fresh oregano	2.5 ml (½ tsp)	½ tsp
sugar	pinch	pinch
dry mustard	1 ml (¼ tsp)	¼ tsp
cayenne pepper	pinch	pinch
garlic, crushed (optional)	1 clove	1 clove

Place all the ingredients in a bowl and whisk to combine thoroughly. Store in a sealed container in the refrigerator. Shake well before use.

Feta and vegetable salad (page 87) and Blue cheese and anchovy dressing

BLUE CHEESE AND ANCHOVY DRESSING   (Makes about 750 ml/1¼ pints/3 cups)

Great on vegetable salads and makes a delicious dip for crudités.

INGREDIENTS	METRIC/IMPERIAL	AMERICAN
blue cheese, crumbled	125 g (4 oz)	¾ cup
anchovies, chopped	10	10
green pepper, chopped	½	½
celery, cut in chunks	½ stick	½ stalk
onion, cut in pieces	½ small	½ small
chopped fresh parsley	15 ml (1 tbsp)	1 tbsp
vegetable oil	500 ml (18 fl oz)	2¼ cups
white wine vinegar	90 ml (3 fl oz)	⅓ cup
prepared mustard	60 ml (4 tbsp)	4 tbsp
red wine vinegar	45 ml (3 tbsp)	3 tbsp
dried basil	2.5 ml (½ tsp)	½ tsp
black pepper	pinch	pinch

Place cheese, anchovies, green pepper, celery, onion and parsley in a food processor or blender. Add remaining ingredients and blend until smooth.

MUSTARD SAUCE

(Makes about 500 ml/18 fl oz/2¼ cups)

INGREDIENTS	METRIC/IMPERIAL	AMERICAN
dry mustard	45 ml (3 tbsp)	3 tbsp
whole mustard seeds, crushed	30 ml (2 tbsp)	2 tbsp
white wine vinegar	75 ml (2½ fl oz)	⅓ cup
Martini Bianco	60 ml (4 tbsp)	4 tbsp
honey	30 ml (2 tbsp)	2 tbsp
salt	5 ml (1 tsp)	1 tsp
dried tarragon, crumbled	2.5 ml (½ tsp)	½ tsp
eggs	2	2
cream	125 ml (4 fl oz)	½ cup

Combine mustard, mustard seeds, vinegar and Martini Bianco. Cover and stand overnight. Stir in honey, salt and tarragon.

In a double boiler over hot water, beat eggs until very light and foamy. Whisk in mustard mixture and cook, stirring occasionally, until thickened, 20-30 minutes. Remove from heat and chill. Shortly before serving, whip cream to soft peaks and fold into the mustard. Delicious served with grilled meats.

Peanut Sauce
(Makes 350 ml/12½ fl oz/1½ cups)

INGREDIENTS	METRIC/IMPERIAL	AMERICAN
crunchy peanut butter	100 g (3½ oz)	½ cup
water	350 ml (12½ fl oz)	1½ cups
chicken stock cubes	½	½
or chicken stock powder	2.5 ml (½ tsp)	½ tsp
curry paste	5 ml (1 tsp)	1 tsp
garlic, crushed	1 clove	1 clove
cayenne pepper	pinch	pinch

Combine all ingredients in a small saucepan, bring to the boil, stirring all the time. Stir well and use when required.

Spicy Sauce
(Makes about 350 ml/12½ fl oz/1½ cups)

INGREDIENTS	METRIC/IMPERIAL	AMERICAN
tomato purée	200 ml (7 fl oz)	¾ cup
brown sugar	45 ml (3 tbsp)	3 tbsp
prepared mild mustard	15 ml (1 tbsp)	1 tbsp
white vinegar	45 ml (3 tbsp)	3 tbsp
dried mixed herbs	2.5 ml (½ tsp)	½ tsp
soy sauce	15 ml (1 tbsp)	1 tbsp
H P sauce	30 ml (2 tbsp)	2 tbsp
Tabasco sauce	few drops	few drops

Combine all the ingredients, bring to the boil, and then simmer for 10 minutes. Serve hot or cold with hamburgers, steaks or chops.

Chinese Plum Dipping Sauce
(Makes about 300 ml/11 fl oz/1¼ cups)

Great for dipping spareribs.

INGREDIENTS	METRIC/IMPERIAL	AMERICAN
plum jam	300 g (11 oz)	1 cup
dry sherry	75 ml (2½ fl oz)	⅓ cup
ground cloves	2.5 ml (½ tsp)	½ tsp
ground anise	2.5 ml (½ tsp)	½ tsp
ground fennel seeds	2.5 ml (½ tsp)	½ tsp
dry mustard (or to taste)	30 g (1 oz)	⅓ cup

Combine all ingredients, except mustard, in a blender. Add mustard a little at a time, blending well until sauce is as hot and spicy as desired.

Traditional Barbecue Sauce
(Makes 625 ml/1 pint/2½ cups)

INGREDIENTS	METRIC/IMPERIAL	AMERICAN
butter or margarine	30 g (1 oz)	2 tbsp
onion, chopped	1	1
garlic, finely chopped	1-2 cloves	1-2 cloves
celery with leaves, chopped	2 sticks	2 stalks
chopped green pepper	60 ml (4 tbsp)	4 tbsp
canned whole tomatoes, undrained	400 g (14 oz)	1½ cups
tomato purée	180 ml (6 fl oz)	¾ cup
tomato paste	30 ml (2 tbsp)	2 tbsp
bay leaf	1	1
dry mustard	10 ml (2 tsp)	2 tsp
salt	5 ml (1 tsp)	1 tsp
ground cloves	2.5 ml (½ tsp)	½ tsp
ground allspice	2.5 ml (½ tsp)	½ tsp
vinegar	75 ml (2½ fl oz)	⅓ cup
lemon juice	30 ml (2 tbsp)	2 tbsp
dry sherry	30 ml (2 tbsp)	2 tbsp
black treacle (molasses)	30 ml (2 tbsp)	2 tbsp
brown sugar	30 ml (2 tbsp)	2 tbsp
Tabasco sauce	few drops	few drops
chopped fresh parsley	15 ml (1 tbsp)	1 tbsp
dried mixed herbs	5 ml (1 tsp)	1 tsp

Heat butter, fry onion and garlic until tender. Add remaining ingredients and simmer for about 30 minutes. Cool and purée in a food processor or blender. Use as a basting sauce for poultry, ribs, sausages, hamburgers and steaks. Keep refrigerated. Sauce may be reheated and served separately with the meat.

Hot Spicy Mint Sauce
(Makes about 300 ml/11 fl oz/1¼ cups)

INGREDIENTS	METRIC/IMPERIAL	AMERICAN
chicken stock	125 ml (4 fl oz)	½ cup
wine vinegar	125 ml (4 fl oz)	½ cup
sugar	60 ml (4 tbsp)	4 tbsp
chopped fresh mint	75 g (2½ oz)	¾ cup
crushed dried red pepper	2.5 ml (½ tsp)	½ tsp
extra chopped fresh mint	30 ml (2 tbsp)	2 tbsp

Combine chicken stock, vinegar and sugar. Bring to the boil, stirring to dissolve sugar. Place the chopped mint in a bowl and pour hot mixture over. Stand for about 1½ hours, then strain, pressing out all the liquid. Stir in crushed red peppers and extra mint. Serve at room temperature.

RED WINE AND CHERRY SAUCE
(Makes about 750 ml/1¼ pints/3 cups)

INGREDIENTS	METRIC/IMPERIAL	AMERICAN
red wine	500 ml (18 fl oz)	2¼ cups
sugar	60 g (2 oz)	⅓ cup
lemon rind	2-cm (¾-in) piece	¾-in piece
bay leaf	1	1
whole cloves	3	3
whole peppercorns	3	3
whole allspice	3	3
stick cinnamon	2-cm (¾-in) piece	¾-in piece
stoned (pitted) ripe cherries	500 g (18 oz)	2 cups
cornflour (cornstarch)	5 ml (1 tsp)	1 tsp
cold water	15 ml (1 tbsp)	1 tbsp

Combine wine, sugar, lemon peel, bay leaf, cloves, peppercorns, allspice and cinnamon. Bring to the boil, stirring to dissolve sugar. Reduce heat and add cherries. Poach gently until cherries are tender, 5-10 minutes. Remove cherries with a slotted spoon and set aside. Bring wine mixture to the boil and cook until reduced to about 300 ml (11 fl oz/1¼ cups). Mix cornflour with cold water and beat into the wine mixture. Cook, stirring, for about 2 minutes. Strain into a bowl and stir in cherries. Serve warm or at room temperature with poultry and game.

SPICED PEACHES   (Serves 8)

INGREDIENTS	METRIC/IMPERIAL	AMERICAN
canned peach halves	750 g (28 oz)	4½ cups
canned stoned (pitted) cherries	400 g (14 oz)	1½ cups
sugar	150 g (5 oz)	¾ cup
cider vinegar	125 ml (4 fl oz)	½ cup
stick cinnamon	1 piece	1 piece
whole cloves	6	6
whole allspice	6	6
dry mustard	5 ml (1 tsp)	1 tsp

Drain fruits and place in a bowl, reserving juice. Combine half the juice with the remaining ingredients. Bring to the boil and simmer for 10 minutes. Pour over the fruit and refrigerate at least overnight before serving.

LEMON PARSLEY BUTTER
(Makes about 125 g/4 oz/½ cup)

Serve with fish, poultry, beef or vegetables.

INGREDIENTS	METRIC/IMPERIAL	AMERICAN
butter	125 g (4 oz)	½ cup
chopped fresh parsley	45 ml (3 tbsp)	3 tbsp
finely grated lemon rind	5 ml (1 tsp)	1 tsp
lemon juice	20 ml (4 tsp)	4 tsp
black pepper	pinch	pinch

Beat butter to soften, then mix in remaining ingredients. Shape into a roll and wrap in foil. Chill, then cut into slices to serve. Alternatively, heat and serve hot with fish or chicken.

VARIATIONS
Add 5 ml (1 tsp) chopped fresh thyme or crushed garlic.

ALMOND BUTTER   (Makes 250 g/9 oz/1 cup)

A delicious accompaniment to grilled poultry or pork.

INGREDIENTS	METRIC/IMPERIAL	AMERICAN
butter, softened	250 g (9 oz)	1 cup
dry sherry	45 ml (3 tbsp)	3 tbsp
ground almonds	60 g (4 oz)	½ cup
grated nutmeg	pinch	pinch

Combine all ingredients and mix well. Shape into a roll and wrap in foil. Chill until needed, then cut into slices to serve.

PORTUGUESE CHILLI OIL
(Makes about 450 ml/16 fl oz/1¾ cups)

Genuine Portuguese chilli (peri-peri) oil – use it with caution as it is very hot.

INGREDIENTS	METRIC/IMPERIAL	AMERICAN
small dried Portuguese chillies	45 g (1½ oz)	1½ oz
vegetable oil	350 ml (12½ fl oz)	1½ cups
garlic	2 cloves	2 cloves
lemon juice	45 ml (3 tbsp)	3 tbsp
salt	2.5 ml (½ tsp)	½ tsp
black pepper	2.5 ml (½ tsp)	½ tsp
whisky	30 ml (2 tbsp)	2 tbsp

Place all the ingredients in a blender and blend for about 30 seconds. Pour into a bottle and store in the refrigerator.

DESSERTS & DRINKS

Desserts should leave your guests feeling satisfied, not overfed! Select one that complements the rest of the meal and suits the season. Plan your menu so that the dessert can be baked at the same time as your main course, or cooked quickly over the remaining hot coals once the main dish is complete. Alternatively, make the dessert in advance and serve it chilled to provide the perfect ending to a delicious meal. Try our quick and easy recipe for Grilled Fruit or Fresh Fruit Kebabs, or impress your guests with more sophisticated fare such as Crêpes Suzette and Baked Alaska.

Prettily served drinks add a festive touch to any barbecue. Serve these tempting beverages with a choice of appetizers as a start to a lovely meal.

Quince and mincemeat crumble (page 96), Baked Alaska celebration-style (page 94), Apricot spritzer and Margaritas (page 99)

BAKED APPLE SLICES (Serves 10-12)

Indirect . . . 45 minutes

INGREDIENTS	METRIC/IMPERIAL	AMERICAN
Granny Smith apples	6	6
lemon juice	30 ml (2 tbsp)	2 tbsp
ground cinnamon	15 ml (1 tbsp)	1 tbsp
sugar	60 ml (4 tbsp)	4 tbsp
vanilla cake mix	500 g (18 oz)	3½ cups
butter, melted	125 g (4 oz)	½ cup
pecan nuts, chopped	100 g (3½ oz)	1 cup
TO SERVE		
ice cream or cream		

Peel, core and slice apples, then combine with lemon juice, half the cinnamon and all the sugar. Toss well and spoon into a 32 x 23-cm (12½ x 9-in) oiled baking tin. Sprinkle cake mix over apples, patting down gently. Sprinkle with remaining cinnamon, drizzle with melted butter and top with nuts. Cover tin with foil.

Prepare an indirect fire and when the coals are ready, position the pan in the centre of the grid. Cover the kettle and bake for about 15 minutes, or until apples start to bubble. Remove foil, cover the kettle and continue baking until top is browned and apples are tender, about 30 minutes more. Serve warm or cool with ice cream or cream if desired.

BAKED ALASKA CELEBRATION-STYLE (Serves 12-14)

Indirect . . . 10 minutes

A firm favourite with all age groups. This dessert makes an ideal birthday cake.

INGREDIENTS	METRIC/IMPERIAL	AMERICAN
sponge cake	25 × 20 cm (10 × 8 in)	10 × 8 in
orange liqueur	100 ml (3½ fl oz)	½ cup
vanilla ice cream	2 litres (3½ pints)	8 cups
canned peach slices, drained	1.5 kg (3 lb)	6 cups
MERINGUE		
egg whites	6	6
castor sugar	250 g (9 oz)	1 cup
TO DECORATE		
egg shell halves	2	2
flaked almonds	60 ml (4 tbsp)	4 tbsp
brandy	60 ml (4 tbsp)	4 tbsp
sparklers		

Line a baking sheet with foil. Slice the cake in half horizontally and place one layer on the foil. Sprinkle generously with half the liqueur. Cover the cake layer on the foil with a 4-cm (1½-in) layer of ice cream and then with a layer of fruit. Now place the second layer of cake in place and sprinkle with the remaining liqueur. Freeze until required. If frozen solid, stand at room temperature for 15 minutes before covering with meringue.

To make the meringue: Beat egg whites until very stiff, then add the sugar a little at a time, beating until all the sugar has been used. Spread or pipe the meringue to cover the cake and ice cream completely. Make two small nests in the top of the meringue and fit the two half egg shells into these nests. Sprinkle the nuts over the meringue.

Using an existing indirect fire, place the dessert on the grid in the centre of the kettle. Cover the kettle and cook for up to 10 minutes, until the edges of the meringue begin to brown. Remove from the kettle, fill the egg shells with brandy and light. Arrange sparklers in the meringue and light. Serve immediately.

FROZEN MOCHA CHEESECAKE (Serves 12)

INGREDIENTS	METRIC/IMPERIAL	AMERICAN
BASE		
Marie biscuits (cookies)	16	16
butter or margarine, melted	60 g (2 oz)	¼ cup
sugar	30 ml (2 tbsp)	2 tbsp
finely grated dark chocolate	45 ml (3 tbsp)	3 tbsp
FILLING		
cream cheese	250 g (4 oz)	1 cup
canned sweetened condensed milk	400 g (14 oz)	1 cup
ready-made chocolate syrup	150 ml (5 fl oz)	⅔ cup
instant coffee granules	30 ml (2 tbsp)	2 tbsp
boiling water	10 ml (2 tsp)	2 tsp
cream	250 ml (9 fl oz)	1 cup
hazelnuts, chopped	100 g (3½ oz)	1 cup
TO DECORATE		
whipped cream		
grated chocolate		

To make the base: Place biscuits in a food processor and process to fine crumbs. Add melted butter, sugar and grated chocolate. Process to mix well, then press onto the base and sides of a greased 23-cm (9-in) springform pan. Chill while making the filling.

To make the filling: Beat the cream cheese until light, add condensed milk and chocolate syrup. Dissolve coffee in boiling water and add to the cream cheese mixture. Beat well. Whip cream and fold into the chocolate mixture. Fold in chopped nuts. Turn into the prepared pan, cover and freeze until firm, about 6 hours or overnight. Decorate with whipped cream and grated chocolate if desired.

FRESH FRUIT KEBABS (Serves 8-10)

INGREDIENTS	METRIC/IMPERIAL	AMERICAN
large marshmallows	24	24
cubes or wedges of fresh fruit		
ORANGE CREAM SAUCE		
crème fraîche*	300 ml (11 fl oz)	1¼ cups
maple-flavoured syrup	45 ml (3 tbsp)	3 tbsp
grated rind of an orange		
chopped walnuts	45 ml (3 tbsp)	3 tbsp

Thread marshmallows and a selection of fresh fruits (such as pineapple, grapes, strawberries, kiwi fruit, banana, peach, nectarine or melon) onto 8 thin wooden skewers. If using bananas or nectarines, sprinkle with a little lemon juice. Serve with the sauce.

To make the orange cream sauce: Combine all the sauce ingredients and chill until required.

* To make crème fraîche Stir 250 ml (9 fl oz/1 cup) cream and 15 ml (1 tbsp) natural yoghurt or buttermilk together in a jar. Cover and keep warm overnight or for 8 hours. Chill well before using.

ICE CREAM INDIAN-STYLE (Serves 6)

This very sweet ice cream is ideal for rounding off a spicy Indian-style meal. Serve in small quantities.

INGREDIENTS	METRIC/IMPERIAL	AMERICAN
canned condensed milk	400 g (14 oz)	1⅔ cups
cream	300 ml (11 fl oz)	1¼ cups
sugar	100 g (3½ oz)	½ cup
finely chopped almonds	15 ml (1 tbsp)	1 tbsp
finely chopped pistachio nuts	15 ml (1 tbsp)	1 tbsp
canned mango slices, drained	350 g (12 oz)	2 cups
lemon juice	45 ml (3 tbsp)	3 tbsp
TO SERVE		
small biscuits (cookies) and fresh fruit		

Bring condensed milk, cream and sugar to the boil, stirring constantly. Leave to simmer over a very low heat for 25 minutes. Add nuts and allow to cool. Purée the mango slices with the lemon juice and add to the cream mixture. Whisk well, then freeze overnight.

To serve: Scoop into small balls and serve with a small biscuit and a few pieces of fresh fruit.

HOT FRUIT SALAD (Serves 10-12)

Direct . . . 10 minutes

INGREDIENTS	METRIC/IMPERIAL	AMERICAN
canned apricot halves	400 g (14 oz)	2½ cups
canned peach slices	400 g (14 oz)	2½ cups
canned stoned (pitted) black cherries	400 g (14 oz)	2½ cups
grapes, seeded	250 g (9 oz)	1¾ cups
cinnamon stick	1 small piece	1 small piece
Kirsch	100 ml (3½ fl oz)	½ cup
cornflour (cornstarch)	60 ml (1 tbsp)	4 tbsp
TO SERVE		
ice cream		

Using a large cast-iron casserole, pour in the undrained fruit. Add the grapes and cinnamon. Cover the casserole and place it in the centre of the grid over a direct fire. Cover the kettle and bring to the boil, about 10 minutes. Combine the Kirsch and cornflour and stir into the sauce. Bring to the boil and allow to thicken slightly. Remove cinnamon stick and spoon hot fruit over ice cream.

GRILLED FRUIT WITH SWEET & SOUR SAUCE (Serves 6-8)

Direct . . . 12-15 minutes

INGREDIENTS	METRIC/IMPERIAL	AMERICAN
FRUIT		
fresh pineapple	1 large	1 large
firm ripe pears	3	3
butter, melted	90 g (3 oz)	⅓ cup
ground cinnamon	5 ml (1 tsp)	1 tsp
grated nutmeg	pinch	pinch
SAUCE		
sour cream	500 ml (18 fl oz)	2¼ cups
brown sugar	100 g (3½ oz)	½ cup
vanilla essence or vanilla extract to taste	5 ml (1 tsp)	1 tsp

First make the sauce: Combine sour cream, brown sugar and vanilla. Mix well and refrigerate for an hour or so.

Peel and cut the pineapple into 2-cm (¾-in) slices. Peel, halve and core the pears. Place fruit in a cast-iron casserole. Combine melted butter, cinnamon and nutmeg and brush over fruit. Place fruit over existing hot coals and cook, covered, for 12-15 minutes, turning two or three times and basting frequently with the butter mixture. Fruit should be lightly browned and still a little firm. Remove fruit to a serving dish. Serve the sauce separately.

CHERRIES JUBILEE (Serves 10-12)

Direct . . . 15 minutes

INGREDIENTS	METRIC/IMPERIAL	AMERICAN
canned stoned		
(pitted) cherries	800 g (28 oz)	5½ cups
cornflour		
(cornstarch)	15 ml (1 tbsp)	1 tbsp
rind and juice of		
an orange		
cherry liqueur	100 ml (3½ fl oz)	½ cup
brandy	100 ml (3½ fl oz)	½ cup
TO SERVE		
vanilla ice cream		

Drain cherries and place the juice in a saucepan or drip pan. Place directly over the coals and bring to the boil. Combine cornflour, orange rind and juice and add to the liquid. Bring to the boil, stirring all the time, then add cherries and heat through. Warm the alcohol and flambé the sauce. Serve over ice cream.

QUINCE AND MINCEMEAT CRUMBLE (Serves 6-8)

Indirect . . . 30 minutes

INGREDIENTS	METRIC/IMPERIAL	AMERICAN
canned quinces or		
apples	400 g (14 oz)	3½ cups
fruit mincemeat	400 g (14 oz)	1¼ cups
sour cream	125 ml (4 fl oz)	½ cup
orange or lemon rind	5 ml (1 tsp)	1 tsp
CRUMBLE		
self-raising flour	250 g (9 oz)	2 cups
brown sugar	75 g (2½ oz)	⅓ cup
rolled oats	60 ml (4 tbsp)	4 tbsp
ground cinnamon	2.5 ml (½ tsp)	½ tsp
ground cloves	pinch	pinch
butter or margarine	100 g (3½ oz)	⅓ cup
TO SERVE		
whipped cream		

Choose a 25-cm (10-in) diameter round or rectangular, shallow casserole and place quinces in the base. Dot generously with the fruit mincemeat. Spoon the sour cream over and sprinkle with orange or lemon rind.

To make the crumble: Sift the flour and add sugar, oats and spices. Stir to combine. Rub in the butter until the mixture resembles fresh breadcrumbs. Sprinkle over the top of the fruit.

Prepare an indirect fire, and place the casserole in the centre of the grid. Cover the kettle and bake for 25-30 minutes depending on how much heat remains in the fire. Serve with whipped cream.

CRÊPES SUZETTE (Serves 8)

Direct . . . 15 minutes. Cooking (Manchurian) grill

A casual way to present an elegant dish. Have the ingredients in attractive containers and make this dessert in front of your guests once you have cooked your main course on the barbecue kettle.

INGREDIENTS	METRIC/IMPERIAL	AMERICAN
crêpes (page 97)	24	24
SAUCE		
butter	125 g (4 oz)	½ cup
sugar	225 g (8 oz)	1 cup
concentrated frozen		
orange juice	100 ml (3½ fl oz)	½ cup
water	200 ml (7 fl oz)	¾ cup
lemon juice	45 ml (3 tbsp)	3 tbsp
zest of oranges	2	2
cornflour		
(cornstarch)	10 ml (2 tsp)	2 tsp
orange liqueur	90 ml (3 fl oz)	⅓ cup
brandy	90 ml (3 fl oz)	⅓ cup

Prepare the crêpes as directed in the recipe on page 97. Fold each crêpe into a triangle and set aside.

Prepare a direct fire. Fit the cooking grill over the fire and allow to heat. Melt butter and when it starts to foam, add sugar and cook stirring all the time until it begins to caramelize. Carefully pour in the orange juice, water and lemon juice. (The mixture may turn stringy at this point.) Continue stirring until the sauce becomes smooth. Add the orange zest. Combine cornflour with half the liqueur and half the brandy and stir into the sauce. Add the folded crêpes to the bubbling sauce and heat through. Warm the remaining alcohol, pour over crêpes and flambé. Serve at once on warmed plates.

BANANAS WITH CARAMELIZED SAUCE (Serves 6-8)

Indirect; Direct . . . 25 minutes.

INGREDIENTS	METRIC/IMPERIAL	AMERICAN
bananas	12	12
vanilla ice cream		
chopped nuts	60 ml (4 tbsp)	4 tbsp
SAUCE		
butter	125 g (4 oz)	½ cup
sugar	125 g (4 oz)	⅔ cup
orange juice	300 ml (11 fl oz)	1¼ cups
lemon juice	30 ml (2 tbsp)	2 tbsp
brandy or rum	60 ml (4 tbsp)	4 tbsp

Place the bananas in their skins into a drip pan. Using an existing indirect fire put the pan onto the grid in the centre of the kettle. Cover the kettle and cook for 15 minutes. Remove the lid and drip pan.

Arrange the coals for direct cooking and prepare the sauce. Using a cast-iron pan, heat butter until bubbling, then add sugar and allow to caramelize. Now add fruit juices and bring to the boil, stirring until the hard pieces of caramel melt. Add brandy or rum and reheat. Peel bananas and add to the sauce. Heat through and serve with ice cream. Sprinkle with nuts.

BAKED BANANAS WITH SPICE BUTTER   (Serves 6)

Direct . . . 10 minutes

INGREDIENTS	METRIC/IMPERIAL	AMERICAN
bananas	12	12
lemon juice	45 ml (3 tbsp)	3 tbsp
fudge	10 squares	10 squares
chopped pecan nuts	45 ml (3 tbsp)	3 tbsp
butter	60 g (2 oz)	¼ cup
castor sugar	30 ml (2 tbsp)	2 tbsp
ground cinnamon	5 ml (1 tsp)	1 tsp
ground mixed spice	2.5 ml (½ tsp)	½ tsp
ground ginger	large pinch	large pinch
whipped cream		

Peel bananas and brush with lemon juice. Slice the bananas in half lengthways and scoop a channel out of the middle. Crumble the fudge and combine with the nuts. Fill the channel with this mixture, then push the two halves of each banana together. Place the bananas in a drip pan. Cream the butter and sugar and add the spices. Dot this mixture over the bananas, then cover the pan with foil.

Place the drip pan in the centre of the grid over an existing direct fire, cover the kettle and bake for 7-10 minutes, until the bananas are piping hot and the fudge centres melting. Serve with whipped cream.

HOT FRUIT KEBABS   (Serves 8-10)

Indirect . . . 10 minutes. Shish kebab holder.

INGREDIENTS	METRIC/IMPERIAL	AMERICAN
marshmallows	24 large	24 large
a selection of fruit		
TO SERVE		
whipped cream or crème fraîche		

Using fruit such as strawberries, thickly sliced kiwi fruit, bananas and pears, and cubes of pineapple, thread a selection of fruit onto wooden skewers. Intersperse the fruit with 2 or 3 marshmallows per skewer.

To cook: Using an existing fire, arrange the coals for indirect cooking and place a drip pan between the coals. Place skewers into the shish kebab holder and stand on the grid over the drip pan. If you do not have a kebab holder, place a brick on either side of the central part of the kettle. Rest the skewers between the bricks. Cover the kettle and cook for 5-10 minutes, depending on how much heat remains in the kettle. The marshmallows should be warm and soft inside. Serve with whipped cream or crème fraîche (page 95).

RHUBARB AND STRAWBERRY CRUMBLE   (Serves 8)

Indirect . . . 30 minutes

Prepare this in advance, then pop it into the barbecue kettle while eating your main course. If the fire is a little low it may take longer to cook.

INGREDIENTS	METRIC/IMPERIAL	AMERICAN
rhubarb	450 g (1 lb)	4 cups
sugar	250 g (9 oz)	1¼ cups
water	150 ml (5 fl oz)	⅔ cup
strawberries, hulled	300 g (11 oz)	2 cups
CRUMBLE		
plain (cake) flour	75 g (2½ oz)	⅔ cup
brown sugar	60 ml (4 tbsp)	4 tbsp
salt		
muesli or rolled oats	60 ml (4 tbsp)	4 tbsp
ground cinnamon	2.5 ml (½ tsp)	½ tsp
grated nutmeg	large pinch	large pinch
butter	60 ml (4 tbsp)	4 tbsp
TO SERVE		
cream or custard		

Cut rhubarb into 3-cm (1¼-in) pieces. Bring sugar and water to the boil, then add the rhubarb and cook for a few minutes until soft. If very sour add a little more sugar. Remove from the heat and add strawberries. Turn into a shallow 25-cm (10-in) round casserole.

To make the crumble: Sift flour, add sugar, salt, muesli or oats, and spices and stir to combine. Rub in the butter. Sprinkle mixture on top of the fruit.

To cook the pie: Using an indirect fire, place the dish in the centre of the grid. Cover the kettle and cook for 20-30 minutes, depending on how hot the fire is. Serve with cream or custard.

BASIC CRÊPE MIXTURE   (Makes 12)

INGREDIENTS	METRIC/IMPERIAL	AMERICAN
plain (cake) flour	125 g (4 oz)	1 cup
salt	1 ml (¼ tsp)	¼ tsp
eggs	2	2
milk	150 ml (5 fl oz)	⅔ cup
water	150 ml (5 fl oz)	⅔ cup
butter, melted	30 ml (2 tbsp)	2 tbsp

Place all the ingredients, except the butter, in a blender and blend for 30 seconds. Scrape down sides of glass jug and blend for a further 30 seconds. Add butter and blend for a few seconds. Let batter stand for 30 minutes before making thin crêpes in a crêpe pan in the usual way.

MINCEMEAT ICE CREAM TART
(Serves 8)

A delicious alternative to Christmas pudding.

INGREDIENTS	METRIC/IMPERIAL	AMERICAN
CRUST		
Marie biscuits (cookies)	16	16
ginger biscuits (cookies)	4	4
butter or margarine, melted	90 g (3 oz)	⅓ cup
brown sugar	45 ml (3 tbsp)	3 tbsp
FILLING		
vanilla ice cream, slightly softened	1½ litres (2½ pints)	6 cups
prepared fruit mincemeat	400 g (14 oz)	1¼ cups
pecan nuts, coarsely chopped	60 g (2 oz)	¾ cup
cream	250 ml (9 fl oz)	1 cup
brandy	30 ml (2 tbsp)	2 tbsp
pecan nut halves		

To make the crust: Break up biscuits and place in a food processor. Process to fine crumbs. Add melted butter and sugar, mix well and press onto the bottom and sides of a 23-cm (9-in) pie dish. Chill while making the filling.

For the filling: Combine ice cream, mincemeat and pecan nuts, mixing quickly so that the ice cream does not melt. Turn into the crust and spread evenly. Freeze until firm, at least 2 hours.

To serve: Whip cream with brandy to stiff peaks. Spoon over the pie and decorate with pecan halves.

HOT ORANGE PUDDING   (Serves 6)

Indirect . . . 30 minutes

INGREDIENTS	METRIC/IMPERIAL	AMERICAN
margarine	60 g (2 oz)	¼ cup
sugar	125 g (4 oz)	⅔ cup
plain (cake) flour	90 g (3 oz)	¾ cup
salt		
apricot jam	15 ml (1 tbsp)	1 tbsp
egg	1	1
grated lemon rind	5 ml (1 tsp)	1 tsp
milk	125 ml (4 fl oz)	½ cup
bicarbonate of soda	2.5 ml (½ tsp)	½ tsp
SYRUP		
water	250 ml (9 fl oz)	1 cup
sugar	125 ml (4 oz)	½ cup
orange juice	125 ml (4 fl oz)	½ cup
margarine	15 ml (1 tbsp)	1 tbsp
TO SERVE		
whipped cream		

First make the syrup: Whisk all the ingredients for the syrup in a food processor or blender until well mixed. Set aside.

Cream the margarine and sugar, then add sifted flour and salt. Beat in jam, egg and lemon rind. Combine milk and bicarbonate of soda and add to the creamed mixture. Pour into an oiled 22-cm (9-in) shallow round casserole and pour the syrup over.

Using an existing indirect fire, place the casserole in the centre of the grid. Cover the kettle and cook for 20-30 minutes, depending on the amount of heat remaining in the coals. Serve hot with whipped cream.

TARTUFO   (Serves 10)

This Italian treat can be made up to one month in advance.

INGREDIENTS	METRIC/IMPERIAL	AMERICAN
castor sugar	130 g (4 oz)	⅔ cup
cocoa powder	65 g (2 oz)	⅔ cup
instant coffee granules	10 ml (2 tsp)	2 tsp
water	80 ml (2½ fl oz)	⅓ cup
egg yolks	4	4
maraschino cherries, stoned (pitted)	10	10
rum	30 ml (2 tbsp)	2 tbsp
cream	250 ml (9 fl oz)	1 cup
dark chocolate, chopped	80 g (2½ oz)	2½ oz
chopped toasted almonds	80 ml (1½ oz)	⅓ cup
grated chocolate		

Sift sugar, cocoa and coffee into a saucepan. Beat in the water and heat, stirring, over medium heat until sugar has dissolved and mixture is smooth. Beat egg yolks on high speed with an electric mixer until light and fluffy, then reduce speed and beat in the hot chocolate mixture in a slow steady stream. Beat constantly until the mixture is cool. Chill for about one hour.

While mixture is chilling, soak cherries in the rum, then remove cherries from rum and set aside. Add rum to the cooled chocolate mixture. Whip the cream to stiff peaks and fold into the chocolate mixture. Gently fold in the chopped dark chocolate and almonds. Place 10 paper cups in a muffin pan and fill each about two-thirds full. Add a cherry to each and top with remaining chocolate mixture. Sprinkle with grated chocolate and freeze until firm, about 4 hours. When frozen, cover with plastic and foil. Serve frozen.

DRINKS

MANGO DAIQUIRI (SERVES 4)

INGREDIENTS	METRIC/IMPERIAL	AMERICAN
crushed ice	500 ml (18 fl oz)	2¼ cups
rum	100 ml (3½ fl oz)	½ cup
sugar	30 ml (2 tbsp)	2 tbsp
mango pulp	250 ml (9 fl oz)	1 cup
lime or lemon juice	75 ml (2½ fl oz)	⅓ cup
slices of lime or lemon to garnish		

Combine all ingredients, except the lime or lemon slices, in a blender and blend. Pour into stemmed glasses and decorate with lime or lemon slices.

NOTE: Substitute puréed fresh strawberries or peaches for the mango pulp.

FRUIT FRAPPÉ (Serves 10-15)

INGREDIENTS	METRIC/IMPERIAL	AMERICAN
lychee or mango juice	450 ml (16 fl oz)	2 cups
vodka	150 ml (5 fl oz)	⅔ cup
dry sparkling wine	1-2 bottles	1-2 bottles
lemon slices and mint sprigs to garnish		

Combine the lychee or mango juice and vodka. Pour into an ice tray and freeze. The mixture will become a firm slush.

To serve: Spoon 15-25 ml (3-5 tsp) of the fruit slush into a champagne glass and top with well-chilled sparkling wine. Decorate with a slice of lemon and a sprig of mint. Serve with short straws.

MARGARITA (Serves 4)

INGREDIENTS	METRIC/IMPERIAL	AMERICAN
lime	4 slices	4 slices
coarse salt		
fresh lime juice	60 ml (4 tbsp)	4 tbsp
tequila	160 ml (5½ fl oz)	⅔ cup
orange liqueur	60 ml (4 tbsp)	4 tbsp
ice cubes	16	16

Rub the rim and the inside of 4 cocktail glasses with slices of lime. Pour a shallow layer of salt into a saucer and dip the glasses into it so that a little of the salt adheres to each glass. Place the remaining ingredients in a blender and blend for a few seconds. Strain into the glasses and serve immediately.

HARVEY WALLBANGER (SERVES 2)

INGREDIENTS	METRIC/IMPERIAL	AMERICAN
ice cubes	12	12
vodka	125 ml (4 fl oz)	½ cup
Galliano liqueur	45 ml (3 tbsp)	3 tbsp
orange juice	625 ml (1 pint)	2½ cups
glacé cherries soaked in Galliano and orange slices to garnish		

Place ice, vodka and Galliano in a blender and blend until ice is crushed. Pour into a tall jug, fill with orange juice.

To serve, pour into tall glasses and decorate each with a slice of orange and a cherry.

ORANGE WHIZZ
(MAKES ABOUT 750 ML/1¼ PINTS/3 CUPS)

INGREDIENTS	METRIC/IMPERIAL	AMERICAN
orange juice	350 ml (12½ fl oz)	1½ cups
lemon juice	100 ml (3½ fl oz)	½ cup
Rose's lime juice	60 ml (4 tbsp)	4 tbsp
water	100 ml (3½ fl oz)	½ cup
vodka	125 ml (4 fl oz)	½ cup
orange liqueur	75 ml (2½ fl oz)	⅓ cup
crushed ice		

Blend all the ingredients except the ice in a blender. Spoon ice into suitable glasses and fill with the orange mixture.

APRICOT SPRITZER
(Makes about 1.5 litres/1¾ pints/6 cups)

INGREDIENTS	METRIC/IMPERIAL	AMERICAN
fresh apricots, stoned	8-10	8 10
apricot liqueur	100 ml (3½ fl oz)	⅓ cup
brandy	45 ml (3 tbsp)	3 tbsp
Angostura bitters	5 ml (1 tsp)	1 tsp
soda water (club soda)	500 ml (18 fl oz)	2 cups
sparkling wine	750 ml (1¼ pints)	3 cups

Place halved apricots in a blender, add apricot liqueur, brandy and bitters. Purée and then strain.
Just before serving add chilled soda water. Half fill the glasses with fruit mixture, then top up with well-chilled sparkling wine.

APPETIZERS

SPICY CHICKEN WINGS (Serves 6-8)

Indirect . . . 20 minutes

INGREDIENTS	METRIC/IMPERIAL	AMERICAN
chicken wings	18-20	18-20
cherry (baby)		
tomatoes		
fresh herbs		
MARINADE		
mayonnaise	60 ml (4 tbsp)	4 tbsp
tomato sauce	60 ml (4 tbsp)	4 tbsp
Hoi Sin sauce*	30 ml (2 tbsp)	2 tbsp
soy sauce	45 ml (3 tbsp)	3 tbsp
smooth apricot jam	60 ml (4 tbsp)	4 tbsp
wine vinegar	45 ml (3 tbsp)	3 tbsp
honey	30 ml (2 tbsp)	2 tbsp
garlic, crushed	2 cloves	2 cloves
chicken stock	45 ml (3 tbsp)	3 tbsp
water	45 ml (3 tbsp)	3 tbsp
black pepper		

First make the marinade: Combine all marinade ingredients in a saucepan and heat until warmed through. Pour over chicken wings in a shallow non-metallic container and stand for at least 6 hours, turning once or twice. Soak thin wooden skewers in water for 10 minutes, then thread 2 or 3 wings onto each skewer and rebrush with the marinade.

Prepare an indirect fire and place a foil drip pan between the coals. Place the chicken wings on the grid over the drip pan. Cover the kettle and cook for about 20 minutes, brushing with marinade once during the cooking time. Thread a cherry tomato onto the end of each skewer and garnish with fresh herbs.

* Available at supermarkets

SKEWERED PRAWNS (Serves 8)

Direct . . . 4 minutes

INGREDIENTS	METRIC/IMPERIAL	AMERICAN
large prawns		
(shrimps), shelled		
and deveined	1 kg (2¼ lb)	2¼ lb
vegetable oil	30 ml (2 tbsp)	2 tbsp
garlic, finely crushed	4-5 cloves	4-5 cloves
green chilli, diced	1	1
brown sugar	20 ml (4 tsp)	4 tsp
coconut milk*	125 ml (4 fl oz)	½ cup
lime or lemon juice	20 ml (4 tsp)	4 tsp

Place prawns in a glass bowl. Combine remaining ingredients, pour over prawns and marinate for about 2 hours. Soak wooden skewers in water for 10 minutes, then thread two prawns onto each skewer, spearing the tail of the first prawn, then the head of the second prawn, then the head of the first prawn and finally the tail of the second prawn.

Prepare a direct fire, place skewers on grid over hot coals and cook for about 2 minutes on each side.

* **To make coconut milk:** Soak 160 g (5½ oz/2 cups) desiccated coconut in 250 ml (9 fl oz/1 cup) boiling water until water is cool. Liquidize, then strain through a cloth-lined sieve, pressing out all the liquid.

DOLMADES WITH LEMON SAUCE

(Serves 8)

INGREDIENTS	METRIC/IMPERIAL	AMERICAN
vine leaves	35-40	35-40
water	45 ml (3 tbsp)	3 tbsp
FILLING		
rice	60 g (2 oz)	⅓ cup
boiling water	150 ml (5 fl oz)	⅔ cup
vegetable oil	60 ml (4 tbsp)	4 tbsp
onion, chopped	1	1
minced (ground) beef		
or lamb	300 g (11 oz)	2½ cups
salt and black pepper		
beef stock cube	1	1
or beef stock powder	5 ml (1 tsp)	1 tsp
chopped fresh parsley	45 ml (3 tbsp)	3 tbsp
turmeric	2.5 ml (½ tsp)	½ tsp
chopped mint	10 ml (2 tsp)	2 tsp
pine nuts or slivered		
almonds	60 ml (4 tbsp)	4 tbsp
SAUCE		
butter	100 g (3½ oz)	⅓ cup
lemon juice	45 ml (3 tbsp)	3 tbsp
egg yolk	1	1
Tabasco sauce	few drops	few drops
black pepper		
GARNISH		
fresh vine leaves		
lemon wedges		
paprika		

First make the filling: Place the rice in the boiling water and cook for 5 minutes, then drain. Heat half the oil, add remaining ingredients and sauté for 5 minutes. Stir in rice. Oil a shallow casserole, place 10 vine leaves on the base, then wrap remaining leaves, envelope-style, around small spoonfuls of the filling. Do not wrap tightly as the filling will expand when cooking. Pour remaining oil and water over the rolls and cover. Simmer for 45 minutes. Uncover and cool to room temperature, then serve on a flat platter and garnish with vine leaves and lemon wedges dipped in paprika. Serve the sauce separately.

To make the sauce: Heat the butter until foaming, then whisk in remaining ingredients. Heat very gently for a few minutes, whisking all the time. Serve hot.

STUFFED BLACK MUSHROOMS WITH RICOTTA (Serves 6)

Indirect . . . 10 minutes

INGREDIENTS	METRIC/IMPERIAL	AMERICAN
brown mushrooms	12 medium	12 medium
lemon juice	15 ml (1 tbsp)	1 tbsp
vegetable oil	15 ml (1 tbsp)	1 tbsp
FILLING		
butter	30 g (1 oz)	2 tbsp
onion, chopped	1 small	1 small
spring (green) onion		
tops, snipped	4	4
cooked, chopped		
spinach (about 8		
large leaves)	60 g (2 oz)	½ cup
chopped pecan nuts or		
walnuts	30 ml (2 tbsp)	2 tbsp
ricotta cheese	150 ml (5 oz)	⅔ cup
salt and black pepper		
chopped fresh dill	15 ml (1 tbsp)	1 tbsp
grated Parmesan cheese		

Wipe mushrooms with a damp cloth. Remove stalks, chop them and set aside. Combine lemon juice and oil and toss mushrooms in this mixture. Arrange mushrooms on a double sheet of foil.

To prepare the filling: Heat butter, add onion and chopped mushroom stalks and sauté for a few minutes. Add spring onion, spinach and nuts, and cook over a high heat to reduce any moisture. Remove from the heat, add ricotta cheese, seasonings and dill. Divide the filling between the mushrooms and sprinkle with Parmesan cheese.

Prepare an indirect fire and place foil in the centre of the grid. Cover the kettle and cook for about 10 minutes.

TARAMASALATA (Serves 6-8)

INGREDIENTS	METRIC/IMPERIAL	AMERICAN
white bread, crusts		
removed	6 slices	6 slices
cold water	250 ml (9 fl oz)	1 cup
smoked cods' roe	125 g (4 oz)	4 oz
lemon juice	45 ml (3 tbsp)	3 tbsp
onion	1 slice	1 slice
garlic	1-2 cloves	1-2 cloves
vegetable oil	150 ml (5 fl oz)	⅔ cup
black pepper		
French bread to serve		

Soak bread in cold water for 5 minutes, then gently squeeze dry. Place in a blender with roe, lemon juice, onion and garlic. With the machine running, slowly add the oil until the mixture is thick and smooth. Season lightly with pepper. Chill, then serve with French bread.

BAKED FETA CHEESE (Serves 4)

Direct . . . 10 minutes

INGREDIENTS	METRIC/IMPERIAL	AMERICAN
feta cheese	225 g (8 oz)	8 oz
Italian olive oil	15 ml (1 tbsp)	1 tbsp
chopped fresh herbs	5 ml (1 tsp)	1 tsp
French bread, sliced		

Place the cheese in the freezer for 1 hour, then onto a large double sheet of heavy-duty foil, curving up the edges so as to prevent the juice from running out. Drizzle with the oil and sprinkle with the herbs. Arrange the bread around the cheese.

Prepare a direct fire, and then place the foil on the grid. Cover the kettle and cook for 7-10 minutes, until cheese is piping hot and beginning to melt.

NOTE: A heavy cast-iron frying pan makes an ideal substitute for the foil.

LIVER, BACON & ONION SKEWERS (Serves 6)

Direct . . . 8 minutes

INGREDIENTS	METRIC/IMPERIAL	AMERICAN
streaky bacon, rinds		
removed	12 rashers	12 slices
calf's liver, sliced		
12-mm (½ -in)		
thick	1 kg (2¼ lb)	2¼ lb
salt and pepper		
baby (pearl or		
pickling) onions,		
cooked	500 g (18 oz)	3½ cups
vegetable oil	45 ml (3 tbsp)	3 tbsp
grainy mustard	15 ml (1 tbsp)	1 tbsp
red wine	45 ml (3 tbsp)	3 tbsp

Partially cook the bacon until it is just beginning to brown, but is still limp. Drain well on paper towel. Cut slices of liver into 2-cm (¾ -in) pieces and sprinkle with salt and pepper.

To prepare skewers: Soak skewers in water for 10 minutes. Onto each skewer thread one end of a bacon strip, then a piece of liver, more bacon, then an onion. Repeat so that each of six skewers has bacon forming 'S' curves around the meat and onions. Combine oil, mustard and red wine, mixing well. Brush over the skewers and stand for 30 minutes.

Prepare a direct fire, oil the grid lightly and place skewers over medium coals. Cook, turning often and brushing with the oil mixture, for 6-8 minutes, or until bacon is crisp and liver is just cooked.

MARINATED GIANT MUSHROOMS
(Serves 4-6)

Direct . . . 4-6 minutes

INGREDIENTS	METRIC/IMPERIAL	AMERICAN
large black mushrooms	750 g (1½ lb)	1½ lb
vegetable oil	125 ml (4 fl oz)	½ cup
red wine	60 ml (4 tbsp)	4 tbsp
lemon juice	10 ml (2 tsp)	2 tsp
garlic, finely crushed	4 cloves	4 cloves
chopped fresh thyme	15 ml (1 tbsp)	1 tbsp
chopped fresh parsley	60 ml (4 tbsp)	4 tbsp
salt and pepper		

Wipe mushrooms with a damp cloth. Combine oil, wine, lemon juice, garlic, thyme and mushrooms. Mix to coat thoroughly and stand for 1 hour.

Prepare a direct fire and when heat is medium high, add drained mushrooms. Cook, uncovered, for 4-6 minutes, turning as needed, until mushrooms are tender. Remove from kettle, sprinkle with chopped parsley, salt and pepper and serve immediately with crusty French bread.

OYSTERS ROCKEFELLER (Serves 4)

Indirect . . . 15 minutes

Prepare the basics in advance. Just before you are ready to eat, place the oysters in the kettle to heat through.

INGREDIENTS	METRIC/IMPERIAL	AMERICAN
oysters, opened	24	24
coarse salt	about 500 g (18 oz)	about 1½ cups
lemon juice	30 ml (2 tbsp)	2 tbsp
Worcestershire sauce		
black pepper		
bacon, cooked and crumbled	4-6 rashers	4-6 slices
chopped fresh parsley	15 ml (1 tbsp)	1 tbsp
Parmesan cheese	45 ml (3 tbsp)	3 tbsp
SPINACH LAYER		
spinach, cooked	250 g (9 oz)	1¼ cups
butter	15 g (½ oz)	1 tbsp
chopped onion	15 ml (1 tbsp)	1 tbsp
plain (cake) flour	15 ml (1 tbsp)	1 tbsp
cream	75 ml (2½ fl oz)	⅓ cup
salt and black pepper		
VELOUTÉ SAUCE		
butter	15 ml (1 tbsp)	1 tbsp
plain (cake) flour	15 ml (1 tbsp)	1 tbsp
chicken stock	100 ml (3½ fl oz)	½ cup
cream	75 ml (2½ fl oz)	½ cup

First prepare the spinach layer: Purée the spinach in a food processor. Melt butter and sauté the onion for a few seconds. Stir in flour, cream and seasonings, and bring to the boil, stirring all the time. Stir in the spinach and set aside.

To make the velouté sauce: Melt the butter, add flour and then stir in the chicken stock. Bring to the boil, stirring all the time, then stir in the cream.

Remove oysters from their shells and place a little of the spinach mixture in each shell. Pour a layer of coarse salt into a shallow baking dish or foil drip pan. Arrange the shells in this salt, sprinkle them with lemon juice, Worcestershire sauce and black pepper. Add an oyster to each shell and then coat with a little sauce. Top with crumbled bacon, parsley and Parmesan cheese.

Prepare an indirect fire, and place the container in the centre of the grid. Cover the kettle and cook for 10-15 minutes. Serve immediately.

SAUSAGE AND FRUIT SKEWERS
(Serves 6)

Indirect . . . 7 minutes

Equally good served at breakfast.

INGREDIENTS	METRIC/IMPERIAL	AMERICAN
pork sausages	1 kg (2¼ lb)	2¼ lb
pineapple	1	1
apples	2	2
lemon juice		
firm winter melon (cantaloupe or spanspeck)	1	1
BASTING SAUCE		
lemon juice	125 ml (4 fl oz)	½ cup
honey	45 ml (3 tbsp)	3 tbsp

Place sausages in a large frying pan and add just enough water to cover. Bring to the boil, then reduce heat and simmer, covered, for about 20 minutes. Drain and cut into chunks. This can be done the day before, then refrigerate until required.

Peel and core pineapple and cut into 2-cm (¾-in) pieces. Core apples and cut into wedges. Sprinkle with a little lemon juice. Cut melon in half, remove seeds and peel. Cut into 2-cm (¾-in) pieces. Soak wooden skewers in water for 10 minutes.

To make the sauce: Mix lemon juice and honey. Thread sausage chunks on skewers alternately with the fruit and brush with the sauce.

Prepare a direct fire, and then place skewers on the oiled grid. Cook, turning and basting frequently, for about 7 minutes, or until sausages are nicely browned.

EASTERN PORK STICKS (Serves 6)

Direct . . . 15 minutes

INGREDIENTS	METRIC/IMPERIAL	AMERICAN
lean pork, finely minced (ground)	500 g (18 oz)	18 oz
water chestnuts, minced (ground)	6	6
garlic, finely crushed	1 large clove	1 large clove
spring (green) onion, finely chopped	1 small	1 small
soy sauce	15 ml (1 tbsp)	1 tbsp
vegetable oil	10 ml (2 tsp)	2 tsp
fresh lemon juice	7.5 ml (1½ tsp)	1½ tsp
grated fresh root ginger	2.5 ml (½ tsp)	½ tsp
sugar	2.5 ml (½ tsp)	½ tsp
Tabasco sauce	few drops	few drops
salt	pinch	pinch
DIPPING SAUCE		
soy sauce	125 ml (4 fl oz)	½ cup
lemon juice	75 ml (2½ fl oz)	⅓ cup
water	45 ml (3 tbsp)	3 tbsp
garlic, finely crushed	2 cloves	2 cloves
sugar	10 ml (2 tsp)	2 tsp
grated fresh root ginger	5 ml (1 tsp)	1 tsp
cayenne pepper	pinch	pinch
GARNISH		
lettuce leaves		
chopped coriander (cilantro) leaves		
mint leaves		
chopped spring (green) onion		

To make the meat mixture: Combine all ingredients, mixing well. Shape into 12 cylinders about 6-cm (2½-in) long. Soak skewers in water for 10 minutes before inserting through each cylinder of meat.

To make the sauce: Combine all ingredients and bring to the boil. Reduce heat and simmer for 5 minutes. Cool.

To cook: Prepare a direct fire and when coals are glowing and hot, arrange pork sticks over coals. Cook for about 10-15 minutes, turning frequently with tongs, until meat is crisped and browned and firm to the touch. Have each person sprinkle a lettuce leaf with coriander, mint and spring onion. Slip pork off each skewer onto a lettuce leaf, wrap lettuce around the pork and dip into the sauce.

DEVILLED CHICKEN LIVERS (Serves 4)

Direct . . . 10-12 minutes

This popular appetizer can be cooked on the 'side' while your main dish is being cooked over an indirect fire.

INGREDIENTS	METRIC/IMPERIAL	AMERICAN
chicken livers, cleaned	500 g (18 oz)	3 cups
olive oil	15 ml (1 tbsp)	1 tbsp
vegetable oil	45 ml (3 tbsp)	3 tbsp
garlic, crushed	2-3 cloves	2-3 cloves
onion, chopped	1 small	1 small
Portuguese chilli (peri-peri) oil to taste (page 91)		
tomatoes, peeled and chopped	2-3	2-3
chicken stock	45 ml (3 tbsp)	3 tbsp
salt and black pepper		

Place a small casserole dish or frying pan (the handles must be metal) over the fire, and allow to heat. Add olive and vegetable oils and heat again. Add the garlic and onion and stir to coat. Cover the kettle and cook for 5 minutes. Add livers, and sauté for a few minutes. Now add the remaining ingredients, cover the kettle and allow to cook for about 7 minutes. Stir well and serve with plenty of French bread.

CHICKEN LIVERS IN RED WINE AND ROSEMARY (Serves 6-8)

Direct . . . 10 minutes. Cooking (Manchurian) grill

This dish is excellent for a large crowd.

INGREDIENTS	METRIC/IMPERIAL	AMERICAN
chicken livers, cleaned	1 kg (2¼ lb)	2¼ lb
butter	150 g (5 oz)	⅔ cup
vegetable oil	45 ml (3 tbsp)	3 tbsp
onion, chopped	1 large	1 large
salt and black pepper		
grated rind of an orange		
chopped fresh rosemary	15-20 ml (3-4 tsp)	3-4 tsp
red wine	300 ml (11 fl oz)	1¼ cups
French bread		

Prepare a direct fire and place the cooking grill over medium coals for a few minutes to heat. Heat the butter and oil, then add onion and sauté until soft. Add livers, seasonings, orange rind and rosemary, and stir for a few minutes. Add the red wine, stir to combine, then cover the kettle and cook for 5 minutes. Serve with plenty of French bread.

BREADS & BATTERS

HERB CASSEROLE BREAD (Makes 1 loaf)

Indirect . . . 50 minutes

INGREDIENTS	METRIC/IMPERIAL	AMERICAN
plain (cake) flour	360 g (12½ oz)	3 cups
instant yeast	15 ml (1 tbsp)	1 tbsp
salt	10 ml (2 tsp)	2 tsp
warm water	300 ml (11 fl oz)	1¼ cups
black treacle (molasses)	60 ml (4 tbsp)	4 tbsp
vegetable oil	30 ml (2 tbsp)	2 tbsp
egg	1	1
wheatgerm	125 g (4 oz)	1 cup
chopped fresh parsley	45 ml (3 tbsp)	3 tbsp
chopped fresh mixed herbs	10 ml (2 tsp)	2 tsp
chopped spring (green) onion	30 ml (2 tbsp)	2 tbsp
black pepper	2.5 ml (½ tsp)	½ tsp
cornmeal (maize meal)	30 ml (2 tbsp)	2 tbsp

Combine two-thirds of the flour with the yeast and salt. Add warm water and beat for 3 minutes. Add black treacle, oil and egg, beating well. Then add wheatgerm, herbs, spring onion and pepper. Beat for a further 2 minutes. Stir in enough of the remaining flour to form a soft batter. Mix well. Generously oil a 3-litre (5¼-pint/12-cup) cast-iron casserole and sprinkle with cornmeal. Turn dough into the prepared casserole and let rise in a warm place for about 30 minutes, or until doubled in bulk.

Prepare an indirect fire and place the casserole in the centre of the grid, cover the kettle and bake for 45-50 minutes. Remove bread from the casserole and cool on a wire rack.

PITTA BREADS (Makes 12 small pittas)

Direct . . . 7 minutes. Cooking (Manchurian) grill

INGREDIENTS	METRIC/IMPERIAL	AMERICAN
plain (cake) flour	300 g (11 oz)	2½ cups
instant yeast	10 ml (2 tsp)	2 tsp
salt	5 ml (1 tsp)	1 tsp
sugar	15 ml (1 tbsp)	1 tbsp
vegetable oil	5 ml (1 tsp)	1 tsp
warm water	180-200 ml (6-7 fl oz)	¾ cup

Place flour, yeast, salt and sugar into the work bowl of a food processor and pulse a few times to aerate. Add oil and sufficient warm water so that the dough forms a ball. Process for 45 seconds. Place dough in an oiled plastic bag and allow to rise until double in size, about 45 minutes. Divide dough into 12 pieces and roll out fairly thinly on a lightly floured surface. Place on a baking sheet and cover with plastic wrap. Allow to prove for 15 minutes.

Place the cooking grill over a slightly spread out direct fire and allow it to heat for 5 minutes. Oil grill lightly, then place baking sheet on the hot surface. Cover the kettle and cook for 5-7 minutes, turning after half the cooking time. Remove and allow to cool slightly before filling.

NOTE: When cooking this type of bread dough, the fire should not be too large or too hot.

PEKING DUCK PANCAKES (Makes 20)

INGREDIENTS	METRIC/IMPERIAL	AMERICAN
plain (cake) flour	250 g (9 oz)	2 cups
boiling water	180 ml (6 fl oz)	⅔ cup
sesame seed oil		

Sift the flour into the work bowl of a food processor. Add boiling water and process until smooth. Cover and stand for 30 minutes. Roll the dough into a sausage shape and cut into 10 pieces. Now cut each piece in half. Roll each piece into a 7.5-cm (3-in) circle and brush lightly with sesame seed oil. Place 2 circles together and carefully roll into a 15-cm (6-in) circle. Cover. Heat a frying pan and cook each pancake until the underside is golden. Turn and cook the other side. Remove from the pan and separate the two circles. Cover and keep warm. Continue until all pancakes have been made. Serve warm with Peking-style Duck (page 54).

YORKSHIRE PUDDING (Makes 10)

Indirect . . . 30 minutes

A traditional accompaniment to roast beef, Yorkshire pudding can be baked in the barbecue kettle while roasting the beef.

INGREDIENTS	METRIC/IMPERIAL	AMERICAN
plain (cake) flour	125 g (4 oz)	1 cup
salt	5 ml (1 tsp)	1 tsp
eggs	2	2
milk	300 ml (11 fl oz)	1¼ cups
vegetable oil		

Place all the ingredients, except the vegetable oil, in a blender and blend for 45 seconds. Scrape the sides of the goblet and blend again for another 45 seconds. Cover and refrigerate for 2 hours before using. About 30 minutes before the end of the beef cooking time, heat a little oil in 10 large muffin pans and fill three-quarters full with batter. Place on top of drip pan under the meat. Cover the kettle and bake for 30 minutes until well puffed and a deep golden brown.

WHOLEMEAL TORTILLAS (Makes 12)

Direct . . . 12 minutes

Use the cooking (Manchurian) grill attachment to cook these useful breads

INGREDIENTS	METRIC/IMPERIAL	AMERICAN
wholemeal (whole-wheat) flour	120 g (4 oz)	1 cup
plain (cake) flour	120 g (4 oz)	1 cup
baking powder	10 ml (2 tsp)	2 tsp
salt	5 ml (1 tsp)	1 tsp
vegetable oil	15 ml (1 tbsp)	1 tbsp
warm water	190-250 ml (6½-9 fl oz)	¾-1 cup

Combine flours, baking powder and salt in a mixing bowl. Stir in oil and enough water to make a smooth dough. Turn out and knead for a few minutes, then divide dough into 12 balls. Roll out each ball on a well-floured surface to a 22-cm (9-in) circle. Sprinkle each one lightly with flour, pile them one on top of the other and cover with a kitchen (dish) towel.

Prepare a direct fire and fit the cooking grill. When hot, place three tortillas on the grill and bake, uncovered, until lightly browned, about 2 minutes on the first side, 1-2 minutes on the second. Stack tortillas when cooked and keep warm while cooking remaining ones.

These tortillas can be cooled, wrapped and frozen for several weeks. To use, wrap in foil and heat in a low oven for several minutes.

GARLIC CHEESE FRENCH BREAD
(Serves 6-8)

Direct . . . 20 minutes

INGREDIENTS	METRIC/IMPERIAL	AMERICAN
French loaf	1 large	1 large
Emmenthal cheese, grated	250 g (9 oz)	2 cups
garlic, crushed	2 cloves	2 cloves
cream	60 ml (4 tbsp)	4 tbsp
chopped fresh parsley	30 ml (2 tbsp)	2 tbsp

Cut bread vertically, but not all the way through, into 3-cm (1¼-in) slices. Combine remaining ingredients and pat between bread slices. Wrap tightly in foil.

Prepare a direct fire and when ready, place the French loaf on the grid. Heat, covered, for about 10 minutes, turning once. Serve hot.

SMOKED GARLIC BREAD Spread the sliced loaf with garlic butter, reassemble the loaf and place on a piece of heavy-duty foil. Fold the foil halfway up the sides of the loaf to hold its shape. Do not seal. Place the loaf on the grid, cover the kettle and bake for 15-20 minutes while smoking other foods.

CHILLI PEPPER CORNBREAD
(Makes 1 loaf)

Indirect . . . 55 minutes

Baked in a cast-iron casserole and cut into wedges, this spicy bread goes well with grilled meats.

INGREDIENTS	METRIC/IMPERIAL	AMERICAN
Cheddar cheese, grated	90 g (3 oz)	¾ cup
chilli pepper (or more to taste), finely crushed	1	1
canned cream-style sweetcorn	400 g (14 oz)	1¾ cups
cornmeal (maize meal)	125 g (4 oz)	¾ cup
eggs	3	3
salt	5 ml (1 tsp)	1 tsp
bicarbonate of soda	2.5 ml (½ tsp)	½ tsp
buttermilk	190 ml (6½ fl oz)	¾ cup
vegetable oil	125 ml (4 fl oz)	½ cup
butter	30 g (1 oz)	2 tbsp

Combine all ingredients, except butter, mixing well. Place butter in a 1.5-litre (2¼-pint/6-cup) cast-iron casserole, and heat until butter melts. Pour in the sweetcorn mixture.

Prepare an indirect fire. Position the casserole over the drip pan, cover the kettle and bake for 45-55 minutes, or until a skewer inserted in the centre comes out clean. Serve warm.

POTBREAD (Makes 1 loaf)

Indirect . . . about 30 minutes

Baked in a cast-iron casserole, it is delicious served with grilled meats.

INGREDIENTS	METRIC/IMPERIAL	AMERICAN
plain (cake) flour	425 g (15 oz)	3½ cups
salt	5 ml (1 tsp)	1 tsp
bicarbonate of soda	2.5 ml (½ tsp)	½ tsp
baking powder	15 ml (1 tbsp)	1 tbsp
raisins	60 ml (4 tbsp)	4 tbsp
caraway seeds (optional)	45 ml (3 tbsp)	3 tbsp
honey	15 ml (1 tbsp)	1 tbsp
buttermilk	500 ml (18 fl oz)	2¼ cups

Combine dry ingredients and stir in raisins and caraway seeds, if using. Mix honey with buttermilk and add to dry ingredients. Mix to a soft dough. Turn out and knead lightly, then shape into a round loaf and place in an oiled cast-iron casserole. Cover the casserole.

Prepare an indirect fire, then place the covered casserole in the centre of the grid. Cover the kettle and bake for 30-35 minutes. Check if bread is cooked after about 25 minutes.

PEASANT BREAD (Makes 1 loaf)

Indirect . . . 30 minutes

INGREDIENTS	METRIC/IMPERIAL	AMERICAN
bread flour	375 g (13 oz)	3 cups
salt	7.5 ml (1½ tsp)	1½ tsp
sugar	5 ml (1 tsp)	1 tsp
instant yeast	15 ml (1 tbsp)	1 tbsp
warm water	about 375 ml (13 fl oz)	1½ cups

Sift flour and salt, add sugar and yeast and stir to combine. Pour in water and, using a dough hook, mix to a soft pliable dough. The mixture should be just sticky to the touch. Cover the dough and stand in a warm place until doubled in bulk, about 45 minutes. Oil a flat cast-iron grill or baking sheet and dust with flour. Using both hands, scoop the risen dough out of the bowl and drop it lengthways onto the grill or baking sheet. Allow to rise for a further 15 minutes. Sprinkle top generously with flour.

Prepare an indirect fire and place the grill or baking sheet in the centre of the grid. Cover the kettle and bake for 20-30 minutes. Cool before slicing.

CRUMPETS (Makes about 30)

Direct . . . 10 minutes. Cooking (Manchurian) grill

A marvellous way to make a large number of crumpets at once. Eat them piping hot as they come off the grill. Make sure the fire is not too hot by spreading the coals out before putting the cooking grill in place.

INGREDIENTS	METRIC/IMPERIAL	AMERICAN
plain (cake) flour	250 g (9 oz)	2 cups
baking powder	20 ml (4 tsp)	4 tsp
salt	2.5 ml (½ tsp)	½ tsp
sugar	20 ml (4 tsp)	4 tsp
eggs	2	2
milk	300 ml (11 fl oz)	1¼ cups
water	45 ml (3 tbsp)	3 tbsp
vegetable oil	30 ml (2 tbsp)	2 tbsp
extra vegetable oil		
TO SERVE		
syrup, honey, jam and cream		

Sift the dry ingredients together and add the sugar. Beat eggs lightly, then add milk, water and oil to the eggs. Pour into dry ingredients and beat until a smooth batter forms.

Prepare a direct fire and then fit a cooking grill. Allow the grill to become hot, and then oil well. Drop spoonfuls of the batter onto the grill. When bubbles rise to the surface, turn the crumpets over. Cook for a few seconds more. Serve with butter, syrup or honey, jam and cream. For a change, serve with a savoury butter and grated Cheddar cheese.

BUTTERMILK SCONES (Makes 12-16)

Indirect . . . 20 minutes

INGREDIENTS	METRIC/IMPERIAL	AMERICAN
plain (cake) flour	240 g (8½ oz)	2 cups
baking powder	10 ml (2 tbsp)	2 tbsp
bicarbonate of soda	2.5 ml (½ tsp)	½ tsp
salt	2.5 ml (½ tsp)	½ tsp
sugar	15 ml (1 tbsp)	1 tbsp
butter or margarine	125 g (4 oz)	½ cup
buttermilk	150 ml (5 fl oz)	⅔ cup
egg	1	1

Oil a heavy cast-iron frying pan or griddle and set aside. Prepare an indirect fire but arrange the coals in a circular pattern around the edge of the fire-pan.

Combine flour, baking powder, bicarbonate of soda, salt and sugar. Rub in butter or margarine until mixture resembles coarse crumbs. Combine buttermilk and egg, mixing well. Add enough liquid to the dry ingredients to form a firm dough. Knead gently on a floured surface, then roll or pat dough to 12-mm (½-in) thickness. Cut into rounds. Place the frying pan or griddle over the coals and arrange scones on it. Cover the kettle and bake for about 20 minutes, or until puffed and pale golden brown. Remove griddle and serve scones hot.

VARIATIONS
Bread on a stick (Direct . . . about 15 minutes)
Add a little more buttermilk if necessary to the above recipe to make a soft dough. Divide the dough into 12 pieces and wrap each piece around a thick wooden skewer in a spiral twist, making sure the dough covers one end of the skewer. Place on the grid over low heat. Do not cover the kettle. Cook, turning as needed, until golden and cooked. Slip bread off the skewers and fill centre with butter if desired. *Makes 12*
Herb kettle bread (Direct . . . 8 minutes)
Add 10 ml (2 tsp) chopped parsley, 5 ml (1 tsp) mixed herbs and a large pinch garlic salt to the dry ingredients of the above recipe for buttermilk scones. Rub in the butter or margarine and add buttermilk and egg mixture. Divide the dough into four pieces, rolling each piece into a rectangle. Cut each rectangle into two strips and lay them on the oiled grid over medium coals. Cook, uncovered, for 3-4 minutes on each side. Cut each strip into four pieces and serve hot with butter. *Makes 32*

ROUND BROWN LOAF (Makes 1 loaf)

Indirect . . . 40 minutes

INGREDIENTS	METRIC/IMPERIAL	AMERICAN
plain (cake) flour	175 g (6 oz)	1½ cups
wholemeal (wholewheat) flour	175 g (6 oz)	1½ cups
rye flour*	120 g (4 oz)	1 cup
baking powder	10 ml (2 tsp)	2 tsp
bicarbonate of soda	5 ml (1 tsp)	1 tsp
salt	2.5 ml (½ tsp)	½ tsp
honey	60 ml (4 tbsp)	4 tbsp
buttermilk	375 ml (13 fl oz)	1½ cups

Combine flours, baking powder, bicarbonate of soda and salt. Add honey and enough buttermilk to make a pliable dough. Then beat about 3 minutes more. The dough should come away from the sides of the bowl. Turn out and knead for about 2 minutes. Shape into a flat round and place in an oiled foil pie dish.

Prepare an indirect fire, then centre the pie dish on the grid. Cover the kettle and bake for about 40 minutes, or until done and nicely browned. Remove from pan and cool on a wire rack. Serve warm with lashings of butter.

* Available from health shops

SPECIAL WHOLEMEAL BREAD
(Makes 1 loaf)

Indirect . . . 40 minutes

INGREDIENTS	METRIC/IMPERIAL	AMERICAN
instant yeast	15 ml (1 tbsp)	1 tbsp
wholemeal (wholewheat) flour	260 g (9½ oz)	2⅓ cups
rolled oats	75 g (2½ oz)	⅓ cup
bran	60 g (2 oz)	¼ cup
salt	7.5 ml (1½ tsp)	1½ tsp
cracked wheat	75 g (2½ oz)	⅓ cup
sunflower seeds	60 ml (4 tbsp)	4 tbsp
black treacle (molasses)	30 ml (2 tbsp)	2 tbsp
vegetable oil	10 ml (2 tsp)	2 tsp
warm water	400-500 ml (14-18 fl oz)	1⅔-2¼ cups

Place all the dry ingredients in a bowl and mix to combine. Combine black treacle, oil and water. Add sufficient liquid to the flour to form a soft dough. Turn into an oiled 30 x 10-cm (12 x 4-in) loaf pan. Stand in a warm place for 20 minutes.

Prepare an indirect fire. Place the pan in the centre of the grid, cover the kettle and bake for about 40 minutes. Cool slightly in the pan before turning out.

SAVOURY AMERICAN MUFFINS
(Makes 9-12)

Indirect . . . 10 minutes

INGREDIENTS	METRIC/IMPERIAL	AMERICAN
bacon	4 rashers	1 slices
plain (cake) flour	125 g (4 oz)	1 cup
cornmeal (maize meal)	125 g (4 oz)	¾ cup
baking powder	10 ml (2 tsp)	2 tsp
salt	2.5 ml (½ tsp)	½ tsp
bicarbonate of soda	2.5 ml (½ tsp)	½ tsp
sugar	30 ml (2 tbsp)	2 tbsp
finely chopped spring (green) onion	30 ml (2 tbsp)	2 tbsp
grated Cheddar cheese	60 ml (4 tbsp)	4 tbsp
buttermilk	250 ml (9 fl oz)	1 cup
vegetable oil	30 ml (2 tbsp)	2 tbsp
egg	1	1

Cook bacon until crisp, and then drain and chop. Set aside. Combine flour, cornmeal, baking powder, salt, bicarbonate of soda and sugar. Mix well. Add bacon, onion and cheese. Combine buttermilk, oil and egg, mixing well. Add to dry ingredients and mix until dry ingredients are just moistened. Line a muffin pan with paper cups and fill each two-thirds full.

Prepare an indirect fire and position the muffin pan in the centre of the grid. Cover the kettle and bake for about 10 minutes, or until done.

SAVOURY BEER LOAF (Makes 1 loaf)

Indirect . . . 45 minutes

This loaf is delicious cut into thick slices and toasted on the kettle.

INGREDIENTS	METRIC/IMPERIAL	AMERICAN
self-raising flour	350 g (12 oz)	3 cups
sugar	45 ml (3 tbsp)	3 tbsp
brown onion soup mix	30 ml (2 tbsp)	2 tbsp
beer	340 ml (12 fl oz)	1⅓ cups
Cheddar cheese, grated	100 g (3½ oz)	1 cup

Combine flour, sugar and onion soup mix. Gradually stir in beer and cheese. Turn into an oiled cast-iron casserole, large enough for the dough to rise.

Prepare an indirect fire, cover the casserole with a lid and place it in the centre of the grid. Cover the kettle and bake the loaf for about 40-45 minutes. Remove casserole lid 15 minutes before end of cooking time to brown the top. Turn out and cool on a wire rack.

To toast, slice thickly, spread with garlic or herb butter and toast over direct heat on an open kettle.

MARINADES & HERB MIXTURES

HERB MIXTURE FOR POULTRY
(Makes about 60 g/2 oz/¾ cup)

INGREDIENTS	METRIC/IMPERIAL	AMERICAN
fresh basil	60 ml (4 tbsp)	4 tbsp
fresh parsley	60 g (2 oz)	¾ cup
fresh thyme	30 g (1 oz)	⅓ cup
fresh oregano	60 ml (4 tbsp)	4 tbsp
fresh sage leaves	60 ml (4 tbsp)	4 tbsp
fresh rosemary leaves	45 ml (3 tbsp)	3 tbsp
bay leaves, broken up	10	10

Dry the basil, parsley, thyme, oregano and sage (see To dry fresh herbs opposite), then crush coarsely. Add rosemary leaves and bay leaves and mix well. Store in a tightly sealed container until needed.

To use: Place 30 ml (2 tbsp) of the herb mixture in a sieve. Place the sieve in a bowl and add water to cover the herbs. Soak for 20 minutes, then drain well, squeezing out excess moisture. Place damp herbs over hot coals before adding poultry and cooking in the usual way. This mixture is also suitable for use with pork.

HERB MIXTURE FOR SEAFOOD
(Makes 100 g/3½ oz/1¼ cups)

INGREDIENTS	METRIC/IMPERIAL	AMERICAN
basil leaves	90 g (3 oz)	1 cup
finely grated lemon rind	15 ml (1 tbsp)	1 tbsp
fresh oregano	60 g (2 oz)	¾ cup
or dried	60 ml (4 tbsp)	4 tbsp
fresh tarragon	60 g (2 oz)	¾ cup
or dried	60 ml (4 tbsp)	4 tbsp
fennel seeds	30 ml (2 tbsp)	2 tbsp
bay leaves	15	15

Dry the basil leaves and then crush them coarsely (see box opposite). Let the lemon rind dry, then add to the basil. Dry the other herbs if using fresh. Add to the basil, breaking bay leaves into pieces. Store in a tightly sealed container until needed.

To use: Place about 30 ml (2 tbsp) of the mixture in a small sieve. Place the sieve in a bowl and add water to cover the herbs. Soak for 20 minutes, then drain well, squeezing out any excess moisture. Put damp herbs on coals just before adding seafood and cook as usual.

HERB MIXTURE FOR MEAT
(Makes about 100 g/3½ oz/1¼ cups)

Suitable for lamb, beef and game.

INGREDIENTS	METRIC/IMPERIAL	AMERICAN
fresh parsley	60 g (2 oz)	¾ cup
fresh marjoram,	45 g (1½ oz)	½ cup
or dried	40 ml (8 tsp)	8 tsp
fresh thyme	45 g (1½ oz)	½ cup
fresh basil leaves	60 g (2 oz)	¾ cup
rosemary leaves	45 ml (3 tbsp)	3 tbsp
juniper berries	60 ml (4 tbsp)	4 tbsp
black peppercorns	15 ml (1 tbsp)	1 tbsp
bay leaves	15 ml (1 tbsp)	1 tbsp

Dry fresh herbs (see box below) and crush coarsely. Combine all ingredients and store in a tightly sealed container until needed.

To use: Place 30 ml (2 tbsp) of the herb mixture in a small sieve. Place the sieve in a bowl with cold water to cover and soak for 20 minutes. Drain well, squeezing out excess moisture. Place damp herbs on hot coals before adding meat, then cook in the usual way. Any meats that take longer than 30 minutes to cook will require additional damp herbs about half way through the cooking time.

TO DRY FRESH HERBS Tie fresh herbs in small bunches and hang upside down in an airy place for 3-4 days or dry in the microwave on paper towel for a few minutes.

RED WINE MARINADE FOR MEAT
(Makes about 500 ml/18 fl oz/2¼ cups)

INGREDIENTS	METRIC/IMPERIAL	AMERICAN
dry red wine	375 ml (13 fl oz)	1½ cups
red wine vinegar	60 ml (4 tbsp)	4 tbsp
vegetable oil	125 ml (4 fl oz)	½ cup
onion, sliced	1	1
carrot, sliced	1	1
bay leaf	1	1
black peppercorns, crushed	5 ml (1 tsp)	1 tsp
chopped fresh thyme	10 ml (2 tsp)	2 tsp

Combine all ingredients, mixing well, and use to marinate beef or venison for up to 24 hours.

VARIATIONS
For lamb: Add 15 ml (1 tbsp) chopped fresh mint and 10 ml (2 tsp) chopped fresh rosemary to the basic marinade.
For poultry or pork: Add 10 ml (2 tsp) chopped fresh sage and 1 chopped apple to the basic marinade.

LEMON MARINADE
(Makes about 250 ml/9 fl oz/1 cup)

INGREDIENTS	METRIC/IMPERIAL	AMERICAN
vegetable oil	125 ml (4 fl oz)	½ cup
juice of lemons	2	2
dry white wine	60 ml (4 tbsp)	4 tbsp
garlic, chopped	1 clove	1 clove
dried sage	5 ml (1 tsp)	1 tsp
grated rind of 1 lemon		
bay leaf	1	1
white pepper	pinch	pinch

Combine all ingredients and beat well. Marinate chicken or veal in a non-metallic container for about 30 minutes before cooking.

VARIATION
For seafood: Substitute 5 ml (1 tsp) dried dill for the dried sage.

DRY MARINADE   (Makes 25 ml/5 tsp)

INGREDIENTS	METRIC/IMPERIAL	AMERICAN
bay leaves	3-4	3-4
ground cloves	pinch	pinch
mace	1 piece	1 piece
grated nutmeg	2.5 ml (½ tsp)	½ tsp
dried thyme	2.5 ml (½ tsp)	½ tsp
paprika	5 ml (1 tsp)	1 tsp
dried chillies	2.5 ml (½ tsp)	½ tsp
whole allspice	1 ml (¼ tsp)	¼ tsp
ground cinnamon	1 ml (¼ tsp)	¼ tsp
dried basil	1 ml (¼ tsp)	¼ tsp
dried oregano	1 ml (¼ tsp)	¼ tsp
black peppercorns	1 ml (¼ tsp)	¼ tsp

Grind all the ingredients together in a spice mill, liquidizer or in a pestle and mortar. Store in an airtight container.
   To use: Rub onto beef, pork or chicken before cooking.

COOKING CHARTS

ROAST BEEF

Cut of meat	Approx. minutes per 450 g/1 lb		
	Rare	Medium	Well done
Fillet	10	12-14	16-18
Rib or sirloin	18-20	20-25	25-30
Rolled beef	20-22	24-26	26-28
Rump	15-18	20-24	26-30

INTERNAL TEMPERATURE
for rare 60-65 °C (140-150 °F)
for medium 60-70 °C (140-160 °F)
for well done 70-75 °C (160-170 °F)

ROAST PORK

Cut of meat	Approx. minutes per 450 g/1 lb
Leg	30-35
Loin	22-25
Shoulder	25-28
Fillet	18-20
Ham (raw)	28-30 plus glazing

INTERNAL TEMPERATURE
70-75 °C (160-170 °F)

MEAT THERMOMETER: Insert a meat thermometer into the thickest part of the meat, taking care that it does not touch any bone as this will give you a false reading. As thermometers may shatter under the fierce heat generated by the barbecue kettle, it is preferable to insert the thermometer when you think the meat is cooked.

ROAST LAMB

Cut of meat	Approx. minutes per 450 g/1 lb	
	Medium	Well done
Crown	22-25	25-28
Leg	18-22	22-28
Loin	15-18	20-22
Shoulder	20-22	24-26
Rack	17-19	21-23

INTERNAL TEMPERATURE
for medium 60-70 °C (140-160 °F)
for well done 70-75 °C (160-170 °F)

POULTRY

Type	Weight	Approx. minutes per 450 g/1 lb
Baby chickens	400 g (14 oz)	40
Chicken	1.5-2 kg (3-4½ lb)	18-20
Duck	2 kg (4½ lb)	20-23
Goose	3 kg (7 lb)	30
Turkey	4 kg (9 lb)	20

INTERNAL TEMPERATURE
80-85 °C (175-185 °F)

NOTE: Be sure to thaw poultry completely before cooking. Thaw turkey in the refrigerator over 2 days, rather than quickly in the heat of the kitchen.

POPULAR ACCESSORIES

CONDIMENT HOLDER fits on the side of the kettle and keeps the salt, pepper, basting brushes and so on close at hand.

CORN 'N' TATER HOLDER is a nickel-plated ring which fits around the outside edge of the barbecue kettle. Potatoes and sweetcorn cook perfectly on this and take up a minimum amount of space.

CHARCOAL CHEST Ideally use a heavy-duty plastic all-weather container that fits under the barbecue kettle for storing and keeping briquettes dry.

CHARCOAL RAILS fit onto the bottom grid and keep the coals in place when cooking by the indirect method.

DRIP PANS Heavy-duty foil pans are designed to fit between the two fires during indirect cooking. These pans may be lined with foil to make cleaning easier.

GRILL AND TOOL HOLDER fits onto the side of the barbecue kettle to hold the barbecue tools.

COOKING (MANCHURIAN) GRILL This large flat disc of mild steel with a lip around the edge is ideal for frying, stir-fries and baking and is great for cooking for a large crowd. Immediately after purchasing, brush well with cooking oil. After using and washing the grill, re-oil before storing. If treated this way the cooking grill will last for ever; if left untreated it will rust.

ROAST HOLDER is an excellent aid when cooking and carrying large joints of meat. It also makes the transferring of hot meat to a carving board simple.

RIB RACK This nickel-plated rack is suitable for cooking ribs, chicken pieces and large chops. It also increases the cooking capacity of the barbecue kettle by as much as 50 percent.

SHISH KEBAB SET This nickel-plated rack contains six sturdy skewers and snaps onto the cooking grid.

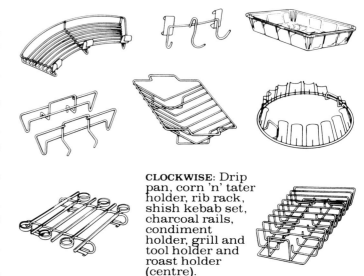

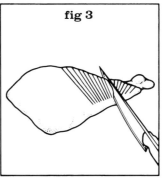

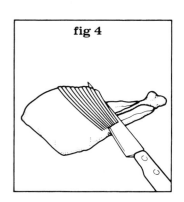

CLOCKWISE: Drip pan, corn 'n' tater holder, rib rack, shish kebab set, charcoal rails, condiment holder, grill and tool holder and roast holder (centre).

MEAT THERMOMETER takes the guesswork out of cooking large joints of meat and poultry by measuring the internal temperature of the food.

CARVING BOARD As food cooked in the barbecue kettle by the indirect method tends to be more juicy than normal, a useful accessory is a carving board with a channel to catch the juice.

TONGS Long-handled tongs are an essential accessory for barbecuing. Use one pair for rearranging hot coals in the kettle and a second for turning the food.

BASTING BRUSH As the heat generated in a barbecue kettle is fierce, having a long-handled natural bristle brush makes sense. Use it to paint glazes, bastes and savoury butters onto fish, seafood, meat, poultry and vegetables.

CARVING MEAT & POULTRY

The barbecue kettle roasts joints of meat and whole poultry to perfection and to carry this perfection to the table, the meat should be presented properly. The carving of the meat is an important part of the presentation and enjoyment of a roast or whole poultry. If done properly, the flavourful juices are saved, and each serving will be tender and succulent. Successful carving requires a very sharp knife and the use of a meat fork or meat tongs.

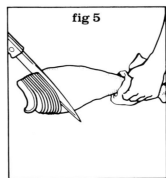

fig 3

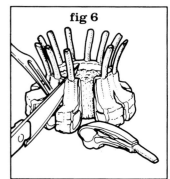

fig 4

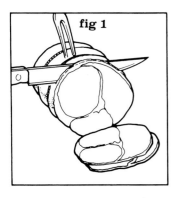

fig 1

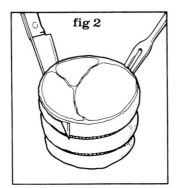

fig 2

fig 5

fig 6

Rolled roasts and boneless cuts

Insert the fork approximately 7.5 cm (3 in) from the right-hand side of the roll. Starting from the right, carve the meat into thin slices (**fig 1**). String or skewers should be removed at this stage. Alternatively, stand the roll upright and insert the fork in the left-hand side of the roll. Starting from the right and moving towards the fork, carve meat horizontally into thin slices (**fig 2**).

Leg or shoulder of lamb, pork, ham

These roasts are alike in shape and have a similar bone structure, so carving is much the same. Always carve at a 90 ° angle to the bone.

Remove several slices from the thin side of the roast, parallel to the length of the bone, so that the joint stands evenly. Now begin carving by making parallel slices down towards the bone, starting at the small (shank) end (**fig 3**). Loosen slices by cutting under them along the bone (**fig 4**). A few slices at a time may be loosened and removed to the serving platter, or the entire cushion sliced, and then arranged on a platter. Turn the joint over and slice round the bone in an almost circular movement (**fig 5**). Cut lengthways down the bone to release the slices, then serve.

Crown roast

This impressive roast is easy to carve. If a firm stuffing, such as minced (ground) meat is used, it may be left intact. If a soft stuffing, such as breadcrumbs or vegetables, is used, remove the stuffing before carving.

Hold roast firmly by placing the fork between a pair of ribs with the tines pointing downward. With the knife close to the rib either to the left or to the right, slice between the ribs from the top of the crown down to the platter (**fig 6**). Allow one or two chops per person.

Standing rib roast

Ask your butcher to loosen the backbone from the ribs. Before bringing the roast to the table, remove the backbone along its entire length by inserting the carving knife between it and the meat. Cut until the knife reaches the ribs beneath (**fig 7**). At the table, place the meat on a platter or board with the ribs pointing away from the carver. Insert the fork to hold the roast steady and, starting from the right, carve the meat into 5-10 mm (¼-½-in) slices across the grain towards the rib bones (**fig 8**). Slip the knife between the meat and rib bones to release the slices (**fig 9**).

Fillet of beef

This is an easy cut to carve. Position the fillet horizontally on the carving board. Carve the meat into slices of the desired thickness. You may wish to offer each person one slice from the thick end and another from the thinner section.

Poultry

Position the bird on its back on the carving board or platter. Remove the thigh and drumstick by cutting between the thigh and the body of the bird to expose the joint. Cut through the joint to sever the leg (**fig 10**). Pull the drumstick away from the thigh and cut through the joint (**fig 11**). Repeat with the other thigh and drumstick. (For large birds, the drumstick can be sliced. Hold the leg upright and remove slices by carving towards the platter (**fig 12**). The thigh can be carved in a similar manner.) Remove each wing by slicing the breast meat close to the wing to expose the joint. Cut through the joint (**fig 13**). Carve the breast in thin slices parallel to the breastbone (**fig 14**). Repeat with the other side of the bird.

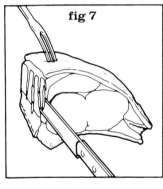
fig 7

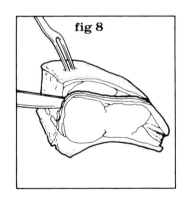
fig 8

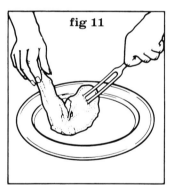
fig 11

fig 12

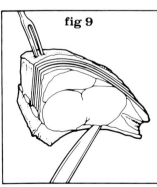
fig 9

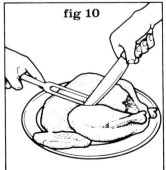
fig 10

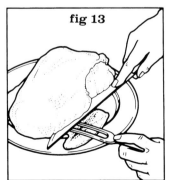
fig 13

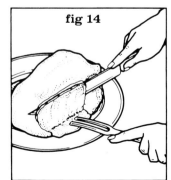
fig 14

INDEX

Accessories to barbecue kettle 110
Almond butter 91
American muffins savoury 107
Angelfish smoked 69
Appletizers 100-103

Bacon smoked 47
Baked beans barbecue 82
Beef
  Bolognese sauce 20
  carpetbag steak 13
  filet au poivre 18
  fillet with green peppercorn
    Bearnaise 13
  hamburgers 20
  island beef kebabs 14
  marinated steaks 14
  meat loaf 14
  pastrami 14
  perfect rump 20
  sauerbraten 16
  smoked ribs American style 16
  smoked roast 12
  standing rib roast 18
  steak fajitas 18
  steak with spicy tamatoe
    sauce 16
  stuffed fillet 12
Bolognese sauce 20
Breads
  chilli pepper cornbread 105
  garlic cheese French bread 105
  herb casserole 104
  peasant 106
  pitta 104
  potbread 105
  round brown loaf 107
  savoury beer loaf 107
  special wholemeal bread 107
  wholemeal tortillas 105
Butter
  almond 91
  lemon parsley 91

Calamari
  marinated 70
  stir fried 66
Carving meat and poultry 110
Chicken livers
  devilled 103
  in red wine and rosemary103
Chicken
  barbecued yoghurt 50
  island 60
  jambalaya 60
  salad grilled 54
  spring chicken
    Portuguese style 50
  spring chickens with sweet
    and sour sauce 56
  stir fry 52
  tandoori 58
  teriyaki 50
  wings oriental 58
  with curry stuffing smoked 51
  with herbs smokey 52
  with mustard and cream 58
  yakitori 52
Cleaning the barbecue kettle 8
Cooking charts 109
Crêpes
  basic mixture 97
  Suzette 96
Crumpets 106

Desserts
  baked Alaska celebration
    style 94
  baked apple slices 94
  baked bananas with spice
    butter 97
  bananas with caramelized
    sauce 96

basic crepe mixture 97
cherries jubilee 96
crepes Suzette 96
fresh fruit kababs 95
frozen mocha cheesecake 94
grilled fruit with sweet and
  sour sauce 95
hot fruit kebabs 97
hot fruit salad 95
hot orange pudding 98
ice cream Indian style 95
mincemeat ice cream tart 98
quince and mincemeat
  crumble 96
rhubarb and strawberry
  crumble 97
Dolmades with lemon sauce 100
Drinks 99
Dry marinade 109
Duck
  glazed 54
  orange and chutney glazed 50
  peking style 54
  with oyster sauce 57

Feta cheese
  and vegetable salad 87
  baked 101
Fish see also Seafood
  baked in salt 66
  barbecued trout 65
  blackened 73
  butterfly style 64
  grilled sardines 68
  in newspaper 66
  marinated salmon 72
  smoked angelfish 69
  smoked trout 69
  steaks with herbs 65
  trout in bacon 69
  with fennel poached 73
Fritters Sweetcorn 83

Game see Guinea fowl Rabbit
  Venison
Gamon roll glazed 42
Goose roast 51
Guinea fowl roast 34

Ham see Pork
Hamburgers on the barbecue 20

Jambalaya chicken 60

Kidney kebabs 25

Lamb
  apple flavoured ribs 24
  barbecued saddle of 30
  chops with mint 26
  coffee glazed leg of 29
  curried kebabs 30
  Greek style leg of 26
  herb smoked shoulder 26
  kidney kebabs 25
  leg in buttermilk 28
  loin of, with blue cheese
    sauce 28
  rack of, with pesto topping28
  saratoga chops 29
  stuffed shoulder, Italian
    style 30
  stuffed, deluxe 29
  sweet and sour ribs 25
  with herbs 24
Liver, bacon and onion
  skewers 101

Marinades 108 109
Mayonaise roasted pepper 88
Mushrooms
  deluxe, black 79
  marinated giant 102
  stuffed black with ricotta 101
Mustard
  dressing 88
  sauce 89

Nasi goreng 40

Oil, Portuguese chilli 91
Onions, baked 82
Oysters rockefeller 102

Paella 70
Pancakes, Peking duck 104
Pastrami 14
Pitta 104
Pizza, giant 80
Polenta 79
Pork
  and orange kebabs 47
  baked ham 45
  barbecued loin of 45
  barbecued spicy loin of pork 38
  Chinese spareribs 47
  chops with barbeque sauce 43
  chops, baked 42
  fillets, piquant 40
  gingered spareribs 46
  glazed gammon roll 42
  grilled lemon chops 38
  grilled schwein hachse 43
  honey-glazed fillets 44
  nasi goreng 40
  old-fashioned baked ham 44
  ribs, spicy 45
  roast leg of 44
  roast loin with apple glaze 46
  roast spicy loin of 46
  smoked bacon 47
  special barbecued ribs 44
  spicy sausagee 38
  sticks, Eastern 103
Portuguese chilli oil 91
Potato
  and bean salad 85
  salad, Eastern 84
  slices, pan-baked 76
Poultry see Chicken, Duck,
  Goose, Turkey
Prawn
  and onion kebabs 68
  Portuguese-style 72
  skewered 100
Preparing the fire
  for direct cooking 8
  for indirect cooking 6
Problem solver 9
Pumpkin
  baked 83
  roast 78

Rabbit, kettle-roasted with
  mustard and brandy sauce 34
Ratatouille 78
Rice
  chow faan 82
  dirty 78
  pilau 83
  salad, Italian 86

Salad dressing
  blue cheese and anchovy 89
  herb 88
  mustard 88
Salads
  chopped Greek 85
  cucumber, walnut and dill 87
  Eastern potato 84
  Feta and vegetable 87
  grilled chicken 54
  Italian rice 86
  peppery bacon green 86
  pineapple 86
  potato and bean 85
  sugarsnap peas with
    coriander 84
  sweetcorn 87
  tangy cabbage 85
Sauces
  Bolognese 20
  Chinese plum dipping 90
  hot spicy mint 90

mustard 89
peanut 90
red wine and cherry 91
spiced peaches 91
spicy 90
traditional barbecue 90
Sauerbraten 16
Sausages
  and fruit skewers 102
  Champagne 12
  spicy 38
  to cook 38
Scones, buttermilk 106
Seafood see also Fish
  barbecued langoustines 68
  marinated calamari 70
  prawn and onion kebabs 68
  prawns, Portuguese-style 72
  rock lobster with herb brandy
    butter 64
  stir-fried calamari 66
Smoking food in the barbecue
  kettle 6
Spareribs
  Chinese 47
  gingered 46
Squid see calamari
Stir-fry
  calamari 66
  chicken 52
  Manchurian-style 76
Successful barbecuing, do's and
  don'ts 9
Sweetcorn
  farm-style 79
  fritters 83
  parcels 79
  salad 87

Tandoori ckicken 58
Taramasalata 101
Tomatoes, baked stuffed 83
Tortillas, wholemeal 105
Turkey
  roast 57
  with ginger-soy glaze,
    spatchcocked 60
  with noodle stuffing,
    Oriental-style 56
  with sherry butter glaze,
    roast 57

Veal
  chops, sage and rosemary 13
  roast leg of 12
Vegetables
  baked onions 82
  baked pumpkin 83
  baked stuffed tomatoes 83
  baked sweet potatoes 82
  barbecued bake beans 82
  black mushrooms deluxe 79
  buttered courgettes 78
  cumin 82
  dirty rice 78
  farm-style sweetcorn 79
  Manchurian-style stir-fry 76
  mixed vegetable pot 80
  pan-baked potato slices 76
  polenta 79
  ratatouille 78
  roast pumpkin 78
  stuffed gem squash 76
  sweetcorn fritters 83
  sweetcorn parcels 79
Venison
  boned shoulder of 35
  kebabs 34
  roast fillet of 35

Yakitori 52
Yorkshire pudding 104